Praise for *Letters to a Young Feminist*:

"Phyllis Chesler has written in language simple, jargon free and direct a series of letters to the young. She is honest about the accomplishments and failures of our generation of feminists, about what she has learned from our efforts and adventures, and her battles won and lost."

—Marge Piercy,
author of *City of Darkness, City of Light*
and *Woman on the Edge of Time*

"A generation ago, Phyllis Chesler addressed the world in the clear, spirited voice of a young revolutionary. Now a wise woman, entirely unrepentant, she still speaks with the same ringing clarity."

—Judith L. Herman,
author of *Trauma & Recovery*

"This is quintessential Chesler—audacious, courageous, tough—but with a gentle undertone of nostalgia for the struggles of her (and our) youth in the women's movement. Feminists young and old have a lot to learn from this book."

—Letty Cottin Pogrebin,
author and founding editor of *Ms.*

"Thank you for writing the book! It's about time somebody set the record straight. It's a splendid book that would make a fine textbook for use in women's studies classes and elsewhere as well. . . . a wonderful, essential book."

—Joanna Russ,
author of *What Are We Fighting for?*
Sex, Race, Class, and the Future of Feminism

"To read this essential handbook is to be reminded that Phyllis Chesler remains one of the great, dazzling philosopher/phrasemakers of both her movement and her time. 'You have a responsibility,' she warns, 'to see that your wounded selves do not get in the way of your warrior selves. . . . Therefore, act generously, not enviously.'"

—Barbara Seaman,
author of *Free and Female* and
The Doctors' Case against the Pill
and co-founder of the National Women's Health Network

"Phyllis Chesler speaks truth to the emerging generations the way I wish somebody had spoken to us when we were young. If you listen, you will hear her bold love and desire to protect us with her hard-earned wisdom and experience. Never again the darkness of ignorance."

—Z. Budapest,
author of *The Grandmother of Time*

Letters

To A Young

Feminist

Books by Phyllis Chesler

Letters

To A Young
Feminist

PHYLLIS CHESLER, PH.D.

FOUR WALLS EIGHT WINDOWS
NEW YORK / LONDON

PUBLISHED IN THE UNITED STATES BY

FOUR WALLS EIGHT WINDOWS

39 WEST 14TH STREET

NEW YORK, N. Y. 10011

U.K. OFFICES:

FOUR WALLS EIGHT WINDOWS/TURNAROUND

27 HORSELL ROAD

LONDON N51 XL

ENGLAND

FIRST PRINTING JANUARY 1998.

LIBRARY OF CONGRESS CATALOGUING-IN-PUBLICATION DATA:

Chesler, Phyllis.

Letters to a young feminist / Phyllis Chesler

p. cm.

Includes bibliographic references.

1. Feminism. 2. Women's rights. 3. Sex role. I. Title.

HQ1154.C464.   1998

305.42—dc21   97-42846

CIP

PRINTED IN THE UNITED STATES

TEXT DESIGN BY ACME ART, INC.

10 9 8 7 6 5 4 3 2 1

Contents

*This work is dedicated to my dearest friend, Merle Hoffman,
whose love and generosity and talent sustained me during
six years of an awful illness.*

Acknowledgments

I thank the staff at Four Walls Eight Windows: Kathryn Belden, John G. H. Oakes, and JillEllyn Riley, both for their creative suggestions and for their publishing vision. I especially thank my intern and first reader, Sanda Balaban, for her steady presence and supremely literate comments. I thank my assistant, and former student, Darlene Dowling, for her steadfastness and devotion. I thank my lawyer, Susan L. Bender for her noble and tender services. I thank Ginny Daly and the staff at Duke University's Perkins Library Special Collections Department where my archives reside, for their bibliographic expertise. I thank my son, Ariel David Chesler, both for his feminist and filial interest in this work. I thank my acupuncturist, Helene Kostre, my chiropractor, Harvey Rossell, my dentist, Michael Iyott, and my internists, David Zimmerman and Susan Levine, for all helping me keep my immune system up and running.

Your Legacy

HERE I SIT, HEAD BENT, writing you an intimate letter. I sense your presence, even though I don't know your name. I envision you as a young woman, possibly a young man, somewhere between the ages of eighteen and thirty-five, but you may also be a decade older—or younger—than that. You may not yet be born.

Perhaps I am trying to speak to my own younger self. When I was coming of age—a process which is still far from over—no one ever spoke strong truths to me in a loving voice. When I was your age, I did not know what I needed to know in order to understand my life—anybody's life. Perhaps, in writing to you, I wish to correct that, to make amends.

In the past, Niccolò Machiavelli wrote a letter such as mine to a prince, Sun Tzu to a king, Virginia Woolf to a gentleman, Rainer Maria Rilke to a male admirer. This letter is for you. You are either poor or rich; you are any or all the colors of the human rainbow, all shades of luck and character. You are my heir. This letter is your legacy. Without your conscious intervention, that legacy may again lie dormant for one hundred years. Or longer.

I imagine you are a person who wants to know why evil exists. People commit evil deeds because we, the good people, do not stop them. To quote Edmund Burke: "All that is necessary for the forces of evil to win in the world is for enough good men to do nothing." Ah, Burke, evil also triumphs when good *women* do nothing.

Men alone are not responsible for patriarchy; women are also their willing, even ardent, collaborators.

Perhaps you believe you can "have it all": a brilliant career, a loving, life-long marriage, healthy children/no children, enough money, and happiness too. If you're anything like I was, you probably believe that whatever awful things may have happened to women in the past, or still are happening to "other" women today, cannot happen to you.

Darling, I don't want to frighten you away, but I don't want to waste your time either, so I can't pretend that simply because you or I *want* it to be so that in fact women and men are equal.

Even when men and women do exactly the same thing, it means something different. The father who changes a diaper is often seen as a hero; not so the mother who is, after all, only doing what she's expected to do. This is not true in reverse. The woman who succeeds in a man's world—although she is not expected to do so—is rarely treated as a conquering hero. She is, more often, seen as an aggressive bitch. She may well be aggressive—but no more than her male colleagues are. Some women try to prove their worth by outdoing their male colleagues in tough, anti-female behavior. Some women feel compelled to behave in "feminine" or "maternal" ways to appease those who would otherwise punish them for stepping so far out of line.

Thus, unlike her male counterparts, the chief judge pours her own coffee, and the police officer may not use what she's learned on the job to stop her husband from beating her; whatever she's learned at work can't over-ride what she's learned all her life about being a woman. The female employee—not her male counterpart—is still expected to buy the gifts, take the coats, bake the cookies for an office party, babysit her employer's child. Hardly gang-rape, but sexism nevertheless.

Yes, the world is different now than it was when I was your age. In only thirty years, a visionary feminism has managed to seriously challenge, if not transform, world con-sciousness. Some astronauts, army officers, ministers, *prime* ministers, and senators are women—there are women's studies programs too, and you can't open a newspaper without reading about some man on trial for rape or sexual harassment. But the truth is women are still far from free. We're not even within striking range.

Fundamentalist passions are threatening to destroy what feminists have accomplished. Three examples immediately come to mind.

The right to an abortion remains under an increasingly bloody siege.

Although we now understand that rape is epidemic and has lasting consequences, we are, as yet, unable to stop it. Today, in Algeria, Bangladesh, Bosnia, Guatemala, Haiti, Rwanda, rape has become a systematic, full-fledged weapon—not merely a spoil—of war. In an era of ethnic cleansing, rape is a form of gender cleansing.

We remain separate and unequal—segregated both by race and gender. In the 1950s and 1960s, brave, young, African-American school children were confronted with adult faces contorted with rage, verbal abuse, turned backs, and hate-filled hearts when they integrated previously all-white schools. Today, brave young women are facing similar fury and danger for trying to integrate traditionally male-only military schools such as the Citadel in South Carolina.

In 1995, heroic nineteen-year-old Shannon Faulkner, the first woman ever to enroll in the previously all-male institution, faced the hate alone; she (and many young men) left after a few weeks. In September of 1996, four women were admitted. By December, two women, Kim Messer and Jeanie Mentavlos, and seventy-five men had quit. While all first-year cadets endured sadistic ritual hazing and harassment, the female cadets were singled out and, in addition to all else, subjected to vulgar songs about masturbation, obscene pictures, sexualized physical intimidation, and death threats. One was also set on fire. Like Faulkner, they were "hated out."

The most extraordinary legal victories are only scraps of paper until human beings test them on the ground. As I write, twenty-four young women have been accepted as cadets at the Citadel. Like their African-American counterparts, the women will not be deterred—but they will pay a high price.

As feminists, we learned that one cannot do such things alone, only together.

I want you to know what our feminist gains are, and why you must not take them for granted. (Although it is your right to do so—we fought for that too.) I also want you to know what remains to be done. I want you to see your place in the historical scheme of things, so you may choose whether and how to stand your ground in history.

Hear me: It may be 1998 but, in my view, we are still living in the 1950s. The poet Sylvia Plath (God/dess rest her soul) is about to put her head in the oven again. I am saying that we have not come far enough. We are also still living in the 1930s, and that great writer, Virginia Woolf, is slowly making her way down to the sea, about to drown herself. No, we are still living in 1913. The sculptor, Camille Claudel, who assisted her lover, Auguste Rodin, on some of his works, is—even as we speak— trussed up and on her way to a lunatic asylum. Claudel was imprisoned in one by her own mother and brother, Paul (the poet). The family condemned her to languish there for thirty years. She died in captivity, in 1943.

I often want to discreetly remove Rodin's august name and replace it with Camille Claudel's in various museums around the world—but then, I'm also the one who wants to behead the statue of Perseus who stands, triumphantly, at the top of the steps at the Metropolitan Museum in New York, holding aloft Medusa's severed head. Her honor demands it, her snaky locks tempt me to it.

There's a worthy precedent for such an action. Did you know that in 1914, while British suffragists were jailed, beaten, and force-fed (they went on hunger strikes) for demanding the vote,

suffragist Polly Richardson marched into a London museum and
swung an ax at Diego Velázquez's *Rokeby Venus*. Society howled.
Velázquez's perfect woman is a reclining nude, and vain too; we
observe Venus observing herself (and us) in a mirror. Perhaps this
was Richardson's way of saying: My Lords, this portrait mocks
real women who are, in fact, powerless. How does it feel to have
something *you* value mutilated and destroyed?

Some say that Plath, Woolf, and Claudel were "mad"
geniuses who'd have ended up the same sad way even if they'd
each been nourished in a woman-loving family and culture.

How can such cynics be so sure?

Although many a sane woman has, in the past, been locked
away in a loony bin, I am not saying that madness itself is a myth.
Madness is real. Neither ideology nor good friends can save a
woman from it. Still, the accumulation of daily slights and humiliations that most women must learn to absorb, to "not see," does
have a way of calling down more than the usual number of demons.

I am thinking about the demands for perfection to which
most girls and women are routinely subjected, combined with
the lack of rewards—in fact, the grave *punishments* that most
women must endure in order to survive. I am no longer talking
only about educated white women of genius with whom you
may be most familiar, but about all women, of all colors, in all
lines of work. So many women are deprived, punished, forced to
walk a far narrower line than most men ever are. Our genius
does not save us, nor does our obedience.

Dutiful women, rebellious women, "mad" geniuses too, so
many of us are systematically ground down and "disappeared,"
rendered invisible, forced to sink out of sight for centuries at a
time. We lose touch with one another in our own lifetimes.

If we cannot see each other, we cannot see ourselves.

You must stand on our feminist shoulders in order to go further than we did.

Confinement distorts character. Centuries of women have been swallowed whole and doomed to such darkness that, like prisoners, we instinctively come to fear the light; it is blinding, unnatural. We fear standing up, we take small and careful steps when we do, we stumble, and we look to our jailors for protection.

Stand up as early as you can in life. Take up as much space in the (male) universe as you need to. Sit with your legs apart, not together. Climb trees. Climb mountains too. Engage in group sports. Dress comfortably. Dress as you wish.

How do we stop injustice?

We begin by speaking truth to power. That child who told the emperor he was naked is one of ours.

We begin by daring to remain connected to those whom prejudice silences, renders less than human.

We begin, of course, by fighting back.

Towards that end, you must move beyond words. You must act. Do not hesitate because your actions may not be perfect enough, or beyond criticism. "Action" is how you put your principles into practice. Not just publicly, or towards those more powerful than you, but also privately, towards those less fortunate than you. Not just towards those who are (safely) far away, but towards those with whom you live and work.

If you're on the right track, you can expect some pretty savage criticism. Trust it. Revel in it. It is the truest measure of your success.

Those who endure small humiliations—daily—say that the most lasting and haunting harm resides in growing accustomed to such treatment, in large part because others insist that you do. After all, *they* have. What's so special about you? "So, your boss asked you and not your male colleagues to make coffee at the meeting— big deal. At least you *have* a job." "So, your husband keeps forgetting his promise to help out with the housework— At least you *have* a husband."

Always implied, but unspoken: "It could be worse." But things could also be better. That will not happen if you do not act heroically.

Telling a rape survivor that she's "exaggerating the trauma in order to get attention" is not useful. Nor is asking her: "Why did you go out with that guy in the first place?"

Comments like these shame a woman into silence and inaction. They imply that there is nothing she can do or say that will change anything so she might as well give up and accept things as they are. Such comments forbid her to storm the gates of power. In a sense, this kind of gatekeeping constitutes bystander behavior. Survivors of serious atrocities say they are haunted by those who heard their screams but turned their backs, closed their doors, remained neutral, refused to take any stand other than an opportunistic one.

One cannot remain a bystander without becoming complicit. Morally, one must "take sides." But, once a person takes the side of anyone who's suffered a grave injustice, listens to her, believes what she says, tries to help her—that quiet act of humanity and courage will be viewed as a traitorous act.

Commit such treason as often as you can.

Women's hearts, men's hearts, are irretrievably broken when people default on the dream of a common, moral humanity (we are all connected, what happens to one happens to all) and do nothing.

I think such interventions are possible when we are inspired by a larger vision, guided by a great dream. Not otherwise.

Women do not need a room of their own. Feminists, both men and women, need a very large continent of our own. Nothing less will do.

Thinking Feminist

WHEN I SAY THAT "WOMEN ARE OPPRESSED," I do not mean that men are never oppressed. Men are, not because of their gender, but because they are *poor* men, or *racially despised* men, or *homosexual* men, or men who do not conform to strict gender stereotypes. Women are oppressed in these ways too, and, in addition, because of their gender.

When I say "women are oppressed," I do not mean that *all* women are oppressed in exactly the same way or to the same degree. There are always exceptions to a rule, but the rule still stands. You must note the rule first, then the exceptions, even if you consider yourself an exception.

For example, most women work for no wages, own less than 1 percent of the world's property, receive one-tenth of all visible income for their paid work, and constitute two-thirds of the world's illiterates. Between 80 and 90 percent of the world's impoverished and refugee populations are women and children.

When we compare women (I think of us as the "touchable" caste) to men, we must first compare women to the men in their own families and class before we compare women to the men in a *less* privileged economic class.

For example, a ruling-class man is groomed to inherit the ships of state or industry; his sister is groomed to marry the right kind of man, breed the right kind of children, excel at hostessing and charity work. Yes, there are exceptions, but they do not negate the rule: most daughters of wealth do not have the same power as their brothers, fathers, or sons.

In addition, most women have at least two full-time jobs. A working- or middle-class woman not only works outside the home for money, she also works, non-stop, when she comes home. She does 80 to 90 percent of the cleaning, shopping, cooking, and child care. If she's lucky, her husband "helps" her. Most working women have less leisure, or stress-free at-home time than their male counterparts.

When women demand fair or equal treatment, we are often opposed, not because we are unworthy or *bad* women but simply because we are *women*. This is a hard lesson to learn.

While poverty and unemployment exacerbate family violence, gender crimes have no class. Or race. Men of every class, color, religion, and ethnicity verbally taunt, harass, rape, batter, and kill women. Most rapes are never reported, few rapists are ever caught, fewer still go to jail. The majority of rapists are not strangers: they know their victims.

Most men do not harass women on the street—but all street harassers are men. Most men are not rapists—but most rapists are men. Most men are not woman-batterers—but almost all batterers are men. The sexual abuse of children is not a male-only crime—but more than 90 percent of such crimes are perpetrated by men. This is a shockingly high percentage given how little time most men spend with children.

Most burglars are men too. If we oppose burglary, we do not think of ourselves as man-haters. Yet, many women—feminists included—still fear that if they actively oppose male violence they may be perceived as man-hating.

I say: Damn the perception and stop the incest. Keep your eyes on the prize. Do not let a little verbal shaming slow you down. Aim for greatness, not "goodness."

Women are also subjected to a double standard. We expect women, but not men, to live up to idealized standards of perfection, to be Superwomen. When a woman turns out to be a human being, not a god, everyone—including the woman herself—tends to feel betrayed.

We have different, and higher, standards for women than we do for men. If a woman does twenty things right and two things wrong, we tend to hang her for her two failures. For example: If she's been a good enough mother and the sole caretaker of her child for ten years, but then leaves home for a week—we will say she's a monster, a maniac. Let's not give her a second chance or the benefit of the doubt. If a man does two things right and twenty things wrong, those two right things will often redeem him. For example: If he's legally acknowledged a child as his and has sometimes paid child support, but done nothing else, we'll say, "But he's done those two things. And he hasn't abused his child!" The fact that he has completely abandoned his child is not seen as abuse.

Other examples: We still punish women for selling sex, not men for buying sex. Men who beat and kill their wives routinely get lesser sentences than battered women do when they fight back and kill their batterers.

We should not use the examples of people who overcome adversity as a way of blaming those who do not. Thus, some people say, "*She* became a CEO even though she grew up on welfare." Or, "But *he* got off drugs even though his mother abused him and his father was a dealer!" Or, "*She* resisted the temptations of the street even though her mother's pimp began selling her when she was seven."

It is possible for each individual to take responsibility for what she does or fails to do and for us to also understand that such victories only happen in token numbers, that they are victories against the odds, that we must change the odds if we are to have more victories.

Feminism is a way of *understanding* reality, not just a series of things to do. Feminism challenges our predilection for one right answer, one right God, one size fits all.

As a feminist, one can be spiritual or secular. One can lead an outwardly conservative life and yet, in feminist terms, be profoundly radical. So too, feminist leaders (like everyone else) can be sexist, or racist, or class-blind, in either their professional or personal lives. Or in both.

When someone challenges a sacred belief, people often "hear" things that are not being said. They may assume things about the messenger that may not be true: "Oh, she doesn't believe in mandatory school prayer—that means she's an atheist." "Oh, she goes to church—that means she's a blind reactionary." "She's in favor of pornography as a First Amendment right—that proves she's not a feminist." "Oh, she's taking maternity leave—that proves she doesn't care about her job the way a man does."

Feminists of my generation told the truth about women's condition. We were messengers from the past, or from the future. As ever, some people thought that killing, or at least defaming, the messengers was a way of making us and our truths disappear.

I'm counting on you not to do that.

My Life as a Girl in America

THE WORLD IN WHICH YOU HAVE GROWN UP is very different from the one into which I was born.

I may have grown up in America but I was veiled: physically, psychologically, sexually, politically, intellectually. The era was like a fundamentalist country. My family was typical, not unusual—at least, not for an old-world family.

I am a first-generation American, born in 1940, a daughter of Eastern European Jewish immigrants who worked hard to put bread on the table, clothes on our backs, the fear of authorities in our hearts. My paternal grandmother, after whom I'm named, ran a tea shop in Russian-occupied Poland; the Cossacks killed her while she was at work. At the time, my father was only an infant. My maternal grandmother was an orphan who worked as a chambermaid. The fact that my mother and her sisters all worked at home as full-time wives and mothers was viewed as a step up. Before me, none of my kin had gone to college. No one, except my mother, had even gone to high school.

My father was a big-hearted truck driver who rose every morning before dawn and left when it was still dark. Sometimes, he'd swing by before the end of the day, scoop me up, take me out for a ride. To this day, being on the open road as a passenger in somebody else's vehicle remains my treasured, familial place.

My mother was always cleaning or cooking or sewing or shopping or hanging out the wash or ironing or planning and overseeing her three active children's every move. We never went hungry: we were, in fact, over-fed. We lived in cramped quarters—no more than 650 square feet for the five of us, and we lived from paycheck to paycheck. I wore hand-me-down clothing and attended public schools. Although we had no library of great books at home (we did have the *Reader's Digest*), I was educationally very privileged. I studied ballet, drama, piano, Hebrew, and painting. My mother had been told that I was gifted and might suffer terribly without this additional stimulation.

My mother had a will of steel. Perhaps that's where I got mine. She was a non-stop worker. As am I. My mother could have run a small country very well on her own. I think that's what she thought she was doing.

My precious, tiny, beautiful mother was a patriarchal loyalist. But she was the one who took me to all those lessons, waited, and brought me home again. Every day, for years, she picked me up at school, which was on our corner, and brought me home for lunch. She always knew exactly where I was. I knew where she was too—either by my side, or in the next room.

My mother never kissed me—or anyone else for that matter. I cannot remember her ever smiling. She criticized me constantly, yelled at me a lot, hit me sometimes, turned me over to my father for more serious discipline.

My father did kiss me, but he also had violent rages and beat me with his belt.

I was a dreamer, a romantic, not practical. I don't think this has changed. I haunted the public library. I loved to read, I read all the time, and the more I read, the more the world beyond my childhood reality beckoned, twinkling. In books, *anything* was possible. Books saved me, but they also exacted their price. I jumped ship, left my family behind when I was very young. I have since come to understand that absolutely no other family can ever become mine. A very American kind of heartbreak/success story.

I'm not sure I can accurately convey what being a teenager in the 1950s was like. It sounds unbelievable now, even to me. Let me try.

There was no sex education. Not in the schools. Not at home. No adult relative ever discussed sex or normal bodily changes. I found out how babies were made quite by accident from a schoolmate, when I was in the fourth grade. My parents refused to tell me whether what I'd heard was true—only that I must not repeat, out loud, whatever I'd heard on this subject. Case closed.

"Down there" was a complete unknown. When I was eleven, I menstruated for the first time. I actually thought I was dying—and that I'd be blamed for killing myself! Like most other girls, I had to use a sanitary napkin, which was kept in place with a belt and safety pins. It felt like a diaper. When I protested, my mother said that her generation had to use rags, which they'd washed and reused. Of course, I was not allowed to use tampons. That meant you were a tramp.

Back then, most mothers wore girdles and insisted that their daughters do the same. I had huge screaming matches with my mother about this. The shop lady would side with my mother, I'd run out of the store. I absolutely refused to wear one of those huge praying mantis ensembles with steel stays and laces. "If you don't, you'll be considered a tramp," my mother said. We compromised. I agreed to wear an elastic girdle, but I soon gave it up. "You look like a loose lady," my mother said. She was right. My flesh *was* wonderfully loose.

My grandmother, mother, and aunts literally shook themselves into and out of their garments. My father once insisted that he'd never seen my mother naked, and he didn't want to see me going around half-naked, even if all the other girls were doing it.

For years, at night, I slept on big metal or pink plastic rollers to give my hair body.

A lady was not supposed to mind feeling uncomfortable.

I was not allowed to shave my legs; that was also something that only loose ladies did. I was not allowed to wear makeup. Or pierce my ears. ("You'll look like a gypsy.") Or wear pants. For a while, it was the height of teenage fashion to wear a crinoline under your dress. This looked like a hoopskirt. My favorite was a gray felt skirt with a white poodle dog under which I could fit *two* crinolines. I wore this with a wide cinch-waist belt.

Imagine the kind of running and jumping and athletics a girl can do in such a modern hoopskirt. But, we were in training as ladies, not tomboys or athletes. Girls weren't supposed to exercise too strenuously. We might "hurt ourselves," i.e. rupture our hymens, damage our ovaries. No one ever said this. I didn't even know I had a hymen.

I had strict, early curfews. I was not allowed out on dates. I could not sleep at anyone else's house. I was closely interrogated about where I'd been and what I'd done.

My life as a girl in America was a thousand times more free than if I'd been born into a poor family in most other countries on earth.

I fought back. I wore lipstick early. (I stopped, briefly, when every feminist in town did, but it didn't feel right, and I soon returned to coloring my lips.) I wore a tough-looking short jacket. Twice, I went on stealing expeditions with girlfriends at a local five & ten-cent store.

My parents didn't want me to have a bad reputation. We were poor, and my sexual virtue was all (they thought) I had in order to make a good marriage.

They were battling with me for my soul—and for my survival. I won, they lost; we all won, we all lost. I became boy crazy anyway.

Then, there was the rest of The Program.

In the 1950s, women were mainly supposed to be wives and mothers. This was the decade in which Rosie-the-Riveter moved to tract housing in the suburbs, drove her husband to the commuter train, dressed up for dinner at home at night, prepared elaborate casseroles and Jell-O molds, played bridge, had coffee-klatches and three children, popped prescription tranquilizers, went crazy, got carted off to a loony bin.

Many women worked—they worked like dogs, not only at home, but outside the home for little money, in dead-end, no-benefit jobs where they earned far less money than their male counterparts. They worked—but they did not have careers. Not if they were "real" women/ladies. Employment (and the want ads) were totally sex segregated. Women were secretaries—not CEOs, elementary school teachers—not college presidents, nurses—not physicians, manicurists—not police officers, actresses—not astronauts. Most working women cleaned other women's houses, babysat for other women's children. As ever, many women also sold sex to men for money in order to feed their families.

Topics you may now routinely discuss were barely whispered about. Abortion was secretive, dangerous, illegal. So was birth control. They were two of many, many unmentionables. Like equal pay for equal work. Back then, there were no lesbians or homosexuals. That is, no one referred to them as such out loud.

Among the white people I knew, one never spoke of black people either, only "Negroes," a word which was usually whispered. It would have been impolite to call anyone black. Racially, the country was segregated (in many ways, of course, it still is). The fight for integration in the schools and in public places was still more than a decade away. The Holocaust, in which six million Jews had just been exterminated in Europe, was never discussed in my home. Or in my Hebrew school.

If I had wanted to be anything other than a wife and mother, or perhaps, an actress, I had absolutely no female role models or mentors. I knew nothing about my feminist history. My generation would not discover our feminist legacy until we were in our twenties, thirties, even forties.

I hope you discover your legacy much sooner than that.

How to Develop a Strong Self in a "Post"-Feminist Age

IN MY TIME, older women told younger women very little about what it takes for a woman to become whole, stay whole, and survive. If they had, we'd have understood, early on, that our first and greatest search should have been for ourselves, not for a prince (or princess), no matter how charming.

Thus, even though I wrote poetry from the time I was eight or nine, listened to jazz at Birdland, acted in plays at the Henry Street Playhouse from the time I was twelve, and sang with bands all through high school—I still had absolutely no sense of self, no clear plan for my future. I only knew that I had to keep reading and leave home.

I left home for good in 1958 to attend college on a full scholarship. On winter and summer breaks, I wore beatnik black, worked as a waitress at Le Figaro and Rienzi's in Greenwich Village, lived on my own on Prince Street, in an area that would later become known as Soho. I kept a diary. I wrote in it at cafes, wrote poetry there too, imagined I was living as an expatriate in Paris, which I was, at least in my head.

I was flying solo, without an instructor or manual, doing a high wire act without a safety net. No one told me that what I was doing could not be done alone, that I was up against thousands of years of hatred towards women, that I'd have to fuck or marry or hostess for some Great Man in order to be allowed to do my own work. Otherwise, my ideas would probably die with me.

No one in a position of authority ever mentioned that women had faced this dilemma before. No one ever told me that, like men, women are also human beings: complicated, ambitious, larger-than-life.

It would have helped. One can't figure out everything by oneself. I don't want you to have to.

Perhaps you have been told that you live in a "post"-feminist age. This phrase implies that women have already won their rights and currently enjoy absolute (perhaps even too much?) freedom. What may be true is that we are "post" that brief period of time when the media found feminist views fashionable. I am not blaming the media. Indeed, today you can't turn on a TV without having full-blown discussions of women's fears and tragedies invade your living room.

The media does air the problems—but only as entertainment, without any feminist political analysis. That's where you come in.

Take street harassment, for example. By the time I was eleven, I had large breasts, a tiny waist, long dark hair. Thus, from the time I was a pre-teenager, my world was not mine. It belonged to the men who stared, whistled, hooted, grimaced, gestured, and invaded my thinking space as if I were public property. When this happened, I would walk faster, eyes cast down, but understand, I was secretly thrilled. This proved I was attractive, and that I had power over adult men.

I experienced street harassment as if it were a compliment—in much the same way that a woman in my mother's generation still brightens when a man calls her a "girl," or opens a door for her.

When women have lemons, we make lemonade.

In 1951, photographer Ruth Orkin shot a street scene in Italy in black-and-white in which at least fifteen men are captured leering at one lone American girl in a long peasant skirt and sandals. Her expression is at once controlled, trapped, terrified. There are men behind her, men on either side of her, men awaiting her. The photo is well-known.

Orkin's photo is a scene of street harassment. It understates the problem. Over the years, I have traveled in Italy as a woman alone; what happens is far worse than what we see in the photo. I have seen Italian men literally risk life and limb to make their appreciation known to a woman. They half fall out of windows, dash into traffic. They are operatic, outrageous, hot-blooded, infantile—and a pain in the ass.

In my time, catcalls, smacking noises, and offers of money were what constituted "the outside world" for most unaccompanied young women. I could not sit on a park bench and gaze at a tree, listen to a soft rain fall, stand before a magnificent painting for the first time, or read a book in a cafe without being interrupted, or without fearing or hoping that I *might* be interrupted by some male stranger. Only in retrospect do I understand that what I once experienced as reality "heightened" was, in effect, reality narrowed.

I loved the attention. I did not think of myself as prey on the move. I had no way of knowing that such men treated most other young girls like this, that it was not really a compliment.

I felt no danger. I felt invincible. I wanted to be as free, sexually, as boys were. I hadn't a clue that a double standard existed that would penalize me for doing the exact same thing that boys did.

It's nearly a half-century later now. I think street harassment for young women has gotten worse, not better. I think the profanity is more intense, the anger too. There are more young men in packs out there—drunk, high, homeless, insane, abused themselves. I've also seen well-dressed adult men, sometimes in uniform, stare, mutter, whisper, follow, strike up sexually explicit conversations with any young woman who attracts their fancy.

Life in a "post"-feminist age does not mean that street harassment has ended. However, it is more often recognized for what it is and named as such. That's an important difference that feminism has made.

There's other good news, as well. Once the kind of man who harasses women on the street decides that a woman is too old (whatever that means)—poof!—that woman becomes invisible. Like magic, she can walk down a city street and feel as free as she did when she was a child. As I aged, I could choose: silence or human interaction. *I* could take the initiative. I loved it.

Nevertheless, some women of my generation continue to feel that if men don't pay attention to them, they no longer exist.

In 1975, I ran several psychotherapy groups for women who were in their twenties and thirties. I would routinely ask each woman to stand up and describe how she saw herself. Every woman (there were no exceptions) spoke only about her outward appearance and then described how much she hated how she looked. Painfully, painstakingly, each speaker would point out her real and imaginary physical imperfections in scathing detail: too skinny here, too fat there, too flabby everywhere, too many lines, too boyish, too matronly, etc. As a group, we were shocked by the difference between how each woman objectively looked, and how she envisioned herself.

Now, more than twenty years and countless books and TV programs later, the experts say that girls are judging themselves even more harshly today, and at ever-younger ages. Mary Pipher, in her best-selling book *Reviving Ophelia: Saving the Selves of Adolescent Girls*, writes: "In all the years I've been a therapist I have yet to meet one girl who likes her body. Girls as skinny as chopsticks complain that their thighs are flabby or their stomachs puff out. . . . They have been culturally conditioned to hate their bodies. . . . When unnatural thinness became attractive, girls (did) unnatural things to be thin."

My dear, has the Vampire of Patriarchy already bitten you, are you more obsessed with dieting inches off your body than in changing the course of history by even one inch?

The legacy my generation of feminists has bequeathed to you is one of resistance, not compliance. Oppose the extraordinary cultural coercion and peer pressure to judge yourself mainly by your appearance. Do not desert your real self in the misguided notion that the more you empty yourself out, the fuller—i.e., more rewarded—you will be. Do not lose psychological weight, do not vacate the place where you used to live in the hope that He or She or God will fill you up.

In my day, respectable women and girls rarely saw men's hidden stash of "girlie" magazines and French postcards. You, on the other hand, are literally surrounded by airbrushed images of half-naked and fully naked girls and women in seductive clothes and poses. You see these images on television, in the movies, on every newsstand.

If you are not taught to resist imagining yourself as either the Whore of Babylon or an anorectic fashion model, you may become convinced that you are ugly, and therefore unworthy of love.

If you are lucky, it will only take you ten or twenty years to understand and overcome the grandiosity and self-hatred such images are meant to engender. It took me about that long.

My mother—like many other mothers—told me that girls were to blame for pretty much anything that happened to them, and, paradoxically, that men could not be trusted. I hated what she said, I hated it so much that, for a long time, I hated her.

In school, I was known as a "brain." I was also known as a "tramp," not because of anything I did, but merely because I had breasts. I "wanted it all." (Just like the guys, i.e. the human beings, did.) I was, therefore, a trial to my parents, and often shunned by other girls, whose approval I sought in vain.

As a result, I did not have much respect for girls. I thought they were boring, cliquish, Goody Two-shoes. Sometimes, I thought I was one of the guys, other times, that I was Jezebel incarnate.

But my mother was right. She, and all the other mothers who told their daughters that men were untrustworthy, had no idea how right they were.

My generation of feminists was the first in more than fifty years to gather anew the statistics on women's condition. We rediscovered what American feminists knew in the nineteenth century: women weren't represented in the Bill of Rights. Women still aren't—that's what our losing fight for the Equal Rights Amendment was about.

We formed "consciousness-raising" groups and discovered that what we had each thought of as private problems—dislike of our bodies, for example—were common problems, hardly unique. This is what we meant by the "personal is political," namely, that private matters were in fact collective realities that demanded political as well as individual solutions.

Perhaps I was my mother's Avenging Angel after all.

Our mothers may have been right about not trusting men, but they were wrong about the solutions. Their solution was to try to break our spirits and turn us against ourselves. Many mothers taught their daughters to blame the woman, no matter what, and to believe the man, no matter what, especially if he were a father, brother, or son.

Our mothers lied to us about how bad things were—things were worse than they said, worse than they knew. Nevertheless, many women of our mother's generation found psychological comfort in placing their faith in an all-male God and His representatives on earth: clergymen, husbands, presidents, doctors, the entire gamut of male experts.

Our parents and teachers did not tell us to mistrust the experts or to trust our own experience.

My mother believed that a girl could be ruined on just one date, her chance of a good marriage forever compromised. However, she did not teach me any self-defense, I had no

weapons training. She merely told me not to go out at night (as
if rape only happened in the dark or at the hands of strangers).
She, and others of her generation, told their daughters to travel
in groups, stay home, lock our doors, ask who was there before
we let anyone in. Let someone in? What if he was already in,
what if he was your father, uncle, stepfather, brother?

Our mothers (God/dess bless them) did not envision
creating abortion clinics, or shelters for battered women. Our
mothers did not envision a feminist government presiding over
sovereign territory; they hardly believed it possible that a
woman could survive, either economically or psychologically,
without a man.

One can. Know that your struggle for independence may be
difficult, even painful. Remaining in bondage exacts an even
higher price.

The Canon

I CAME INTO CONSCIOUSNESS on my own, mainly through books.

Because I live in my head so much, and in books, what I'm about to tell you is, for me, very personal.

From kindergarten until I was nearly thirty, I, the non-stop reader, knew practically nothing about women writers, painters, scientists, spiritual or political leaders, feminists, union organizers, revolutionaries. If only I'd stumbled upon the writings of Mary Wollstonecraft or Matilda Joslyn Gage, surely they might have strengthened me, given me some self-respect, a clue, some company.

By the time I'd graduated from high school, I'd read Ralph Waldo Emerson and Henry David Thoreau, but not Margaret Fuller or Charlotte Perkins Gilman; I'd heard about male abolitionists—John Brown, William Lloyd Garrison, Wendell Phillips,

Frederick Douglass—but not about Sojourner Truth, Harriet Tub-
man, Harriet Jacobs, Harriet Beecher Stowe, or the Grimké sisters.

Looking back, I think it was a conspiracy—what else could
it have been?

I'd never heard of Aphra Behn—the first English-speaking
woman to earn her living as a writer. No teacher, no book ever
said that the first novel ever written, *The Tales of Genji*, had been
written by Lady Murasaki in eleventh-century Japan. When I
started college, I'd never heard of Virginia Woolf, and when I
finally did, no teacher ever mentioned that although Woolf was
married, she also loved women. I knew about Shakespeare, but
not that his "Dark Lady" might have been a gentleman. I loved
Walt Whitman, I read him all the time, but I hadn't a clue that
he loved men. No teacher ever mentioned that Socrates and
Michelangelo were homosexuals too.

Oh, and now the floodgates of memory open: I'd read
Nathaniel Hawthorne, Charles Dickens, Herman Melville,
Edgar Allan Poe, Fyodor Dostoevski, Count Leo Tolstoi, Jean
Paul Sartre, Albert Camus—but not the sisters Brontë, George
Eliot, Edith Wharton, Gertrude Stein, Colette, Anaïs Nin, Jean
Rhys, Simone de Beauvoir, Natalie Sarraute.

No book, no teacher ever mentioned, even casually, that
Dickens, Melville, Tolstoi, were fierce misogynists. Please understand: I am not saying that a great novel is a "failure" because its
creator abused women or kept slaves. Many men have hated and
feared their slaves and wives, upon whom they were, nevertheless, absolutely dependent; few were great writers. Racists and
anti-Semites can, and have, written great poetry: Ezra Pound and
T. S. Eliot are two examples. The list, the loss, the misinformation,
the defensive cover-ups are endless.

There is a great sadness in knowing that men of genius are not able to transcend the limits of patriarchy. Had I but known that the works I so cherished had been done by human beings, not gods, and that great women, including feminists, had also once lived and worked, I suspect I might have been able to break free sooner from a whole host of fatally misguided notions.

What we don't know *can* hurt us.

Forgetting, not knowing your own story, is dangerous. You will have to reinvent the wheel, fight the same battles again and again, with no guiding role models.

I therefore beg you, if you are able to pursue higher education, do not take the feminist and multi-cultural courses that are offered by the academy for granted.

Empowering role-models were equally scarce in my real life. In eight years of public primary school, I can remember only two female teachers who didn't punish me for my incessant reading during class. In four years of high school, only four of my teachers (12 percent) treated me as if my ideas mattered.

I experienced their respect as the greatest love I'd ever known. Two were women, two were men.

I hope you have at least this much love in your early years. We each deserve a lot more.

In four years of college, I had one female teacher who was both supportive and accessible, and one in my six years in graduate school. I had no female teachers in medical school, which I attended for a year. And, I had no teachers of color, no opportunity to learn, early on, certain truths, certain strengths unknown to most white people.

For a woman of my time, I probably had more teacher encouragement and role-models than most. And that's the good news. By the time I got to college, some of my male professors paid all too much attention to me, asked me out on dates, and threatened to fail me (and other students) if we didn't sleep with them.

Like most female students, I was sexually harassed by my male professors and employers. This attention was both wanted and unwanted—it made me uncomfortable, and it flattered me, too. Like others of my generation, I was bred to accept and enjoy it, and above all to keep quiet about it, forget it, and to blame myself if something about these peculiar arrangements bothered me. For years, in isolation, I did so, until movement in the late 1960s allowed me to analyze my fate in feminist terms.

Like most women, I've had to fend off many unwanted advances. One pays a price for doing so. As every woman knows, Hell hath no fury like a man spurned. Two examples, among thousands: In the late 1960s, after dinner, the head of a department at a prestigious medical school tried to rape me. I was a graduate student and we'd met, at his suggestion (I'm guilty, I confess, I went, I ate), to discuss how he could assist me in getting my research funded. In the decidedly non-amorous scuffle that ensued, I broke his ribs, and although I helped him to a nearby hospital (only women actually do things like this), needless to say, this professor never did mentor my research.

In the early 1970s, another professor, a sociologist, arrived to rate my college's curriculum for a national review board. I admit it, I did it again—I accepted his invitation to a dinner party with Very Famous (white male) Intellectuals and their wives. My equally ambitious heterosexual male counterparts also accepted dinner invitations without—I assume—having to face sexual harassment. However, I had the audacity to reject this man's every subsequent social and sexual advance. He retaliated and arranged for a scathing review of my first book to be published in *Partisan Review*. He got a woman to write it—a woman who years later apologized to me about it.

These two older male professors did not see me as their heir, as a future member of their team; nor were they overcome with love for me. They treated me as they did because I was a woman. It was nothing personal. This is what makes it poignant, utterly heartbreaking—the inexorable lead-weight impersonality of prejudice.

These professors were not unusual. Most men viewed women as pussy: wife-pussy, girlfriend-pussy, whore-pussy. This harassment and lack of mentoring didn't stop me—here I am—but it didn't help me either.

Sexual harassment was so common, so pervasive, so accepted, that it was virtually invisible. The shame, the stench stuck to the victim or to the whistle-blower. The victimizer never experienced the consequences of his actions; he was never named, and when he was, all ranks closed to protect him and to destroy his accuser. In the 1950s and 1960s, the Great Men (and Token Women) of the academy neither named nor studied sexual violence; ultimately, their contribution would be to characterize the 1970s grassroots feminist claims as unscientific and unworthy of funding.

Today, many men are being accused in open court of sexual harassment and rape. Our feminist work has not ended these foul practices, but it has empowered women to fight back—and to keep fighting back. Today, many universities and private corporations have developed policies on sexual harassment. Pamphlets are available. Be sure you read them well.

This is a great achievement and I am proud of it.

The lessons: One can overcome a great deal, including an utter absence of information. Even without role-models. But how much more you may accomplish with some!

Radical Compassion

IN THE LAST DECADE, some have said that the feminists of my generation were obsessed by sexual violence and that, therefore, we opposed sexual pleasure. This is a lie. Some feminists crusaded against compulsory heterosexuality and prostitution, but many of us also sought sexual pleasure with fervor and determination.

Some Second Wave feminists focused mainly on sexual *violence*; they did not want the world to confuse violence with *pleasure*. This group was heartsick, outraged by how often incest victims and abused children ended up in prostitution and pornography; they also focused on the extent to which young children, both girls and boys, were being sold or kidnapped into brothels. This group rarely explored the ways in which women sought and found sexual pleasure.

Other Second Wave feminists urged women to take charge of their own sexual pleasure. This group tended to focus on the dangers of state- or church-sponsored censorship and repression. They viewed prostitution and pornography as forms of alienated, dangerous, but at least paid labor; they urged that prostitution be legalized or decriminalized as a step toward improving the working conditions of "sex workers." These feminists often focused on women who claimed to have freely chosen or who said they enjoyed being prostitutes. Such feminists themselves had—or supported women who were exploring new sexual freedoms, including bisexuality and lesbianism.

However, despite some notable exceptions, few feminists in either ideological camp committed acts of civil disobedience, spent any time in jail, started serious hunger strikes. To my knowledge, no one in either camp managed to launch a military raid to free underage or adult women (and men) who had been kidnapped and were being held against their will in brothels or rape camps.

No surprise here. It is always easier to describe the atrocities than to put one's own body on the line to prevent or end them.

Are you afraid that if you focus too much on sexual violence you'll lose your appetite for sexual pleasure? It is true, many women (men too) who counsel rape victims do, for a while, withdraw from sexual intimacy.

It passes.

There is a difference between admitting that rape is traumatic—and failing to deal with that trauma. There is a difference between conceding that bad things can happen to you through no fault of your own—and letting that fact demoralize you. Atrocities do happen. To many of us. How we respond is everything.

For example, if you have been sexually assaulted, that is no reason for you to continue the dirty work against yourself. The question is, are you willing to try and practice the kind of generosity towards yourself and towards others that may never have been shown to you?

I think both men and women owe women a large measure of radical compassion. Women often withhold this resource from each other, or dole it out as if it were a scarce commodity. And then only to women who do not threaten us. This tells me two things: women are likely to be pushovers for the slightest bit of maternal warmth that finally comes our way; and that women need only a small amount of encouragement and compassion in order to keep going.

With *more* than a little, who knows how far we might go?

There is a great advantage to knowing that, at any moment, you may become a casualty in the war against women. If you know that this can happen—that there's nothing you can do to avoid it—you can learn how to sidestep some blows and endure the unavoidable ones, by keeping your eyes open, maintaining clarity, and naming each blow accurately, for what it is.

You do this to aid yourself in remembering that you have not caused your own pain. It is psychologically crucial that you not blame yourself and not automatically take things personally. The truth is that many so-called personal things are quite impersonal—e.g., being captured by enemy soldiers, never being hired, being first fired, being rejected by your light-skinned family because you are dark, being rejected because you are homosexual or lesbian.

I am not suggesting that you become fatalistic or go limp in the jaws of adversity. While you must understand reality with some detachment, you must, at the same time, learn how to take radical responsibility for what you do or fail to do.

In order for you to help even one other woman you must first become very strong yourself. If you can't take care of yourself—if you don't have a strong self to take care of—you certainly can't take care of anyone else.

You must become radically compassionate towards yourself. Traditionally, women have remained compassionately connected to others who have demeaned, destroyed, exploited, terrorized, or abandoned them. Under such circumstances, it is important to learn how to disconnect.

This is hard, not easy to do, but your legacy is one of ongoing, everyday, evolution and transformation—not stasis. Your legacy prizes freedom as much as happiness, self-love as much as selflessness. Remember that.

An Opening in History

MY GENERATION HAD IT EASY. We had no Rolodexes. We didn't network. We didn't need to. Some of us had been active in the 1960s civil rights and anti-war movements (I was), where we had been expected to make the coffee and enable the men to shine. Some of us came from Ivy League colleges and suburban marriages, where we had been expected to do the same damn things. There was a new spirit in the land, a new organization too: the National Organization for Women. We joined. We were mainly, but not only, white and educated. We'd had enough of being handmaids. We were ready to say goodbye to all that.

One fine day, we opened our front doors and, like Ibsen's Nora, simply walked out. Unlike Nora, we were not alone. There were thousands of women in each city on the move. Overnight, there were thousands of consciousness-raising groups, speak-outs, marches, demonstrations, meetings, campaigns in every major American city, on most college campuses, within many professional associations. It was thrilling, miraculous, unbelievable. The media covered our every statement. Whatever we said was considered news.

We didn't *work* for this; it was ours, an opening in history, a miracle. Overnight, or so it seemed, we formed organizations, ran for public office, sponsored legislation, created rape crisis hotlines and shelters for battered women. Consciousness-raising groups educated and empowered us to enter previously all-male professions. Women became police officers, firefighters, judges, carpenters, lawyers, physicians, electricians, professors, scientists, corporate managers, rabbis, ministers, investment bankers, hard news journalists, editors-in-chief, small business owners. And astronauts. And sports heroes. And armed-forces officers who trained men and flew combat missions themselves.

A far cry from the full-time wives, nurses, manicurists, secretaries, shop girls, gossip columnists, actresses, and grade-school teachers of my childhood.

I don't know what kind of life I would have been if there had been no modern feminist movement; a lesser life; a more miserable one, I'm sure. I'll never forget how life gained its fourth dimension, in 1967, when suddenly, the world was bursting with brave, bold, beautiful, adventurous creatures, most of them women. And feminists. It was amazing!

Sure, we Second Wave feminist had more "fun" in the late 1960s. We were young and felt invincible. We had no idea that this struggle would take a lifetime and be much harder than anyone thought. Holding one's own against patriarchy, just holding one's own is not easy. Resisting it—building a resistance movement—would take all we had.

Women's entrance into higher paying jobs did not come easily. Once we became conscious, we still had to fight unimaginably hard for each small gain. But we had each other, which made all the difference. It made having to fight—which we often experienced as "losing"—bearable, possible. Those employers who had refused to hire women in the first place were not happy to do so after we had legally forced their hands. Contrary to most myths about affirmative action, which claim that having quotas lowers standards, most women were in fact over-qualified. Often, a woman has to be twice as good as a man and willing to work twice as hard in a hostile atmosphere in order to keep her job. That is one of the many unwritten job descriptions for women.

In the 1970s, I knew women tunnel builders (sandhogs) in New York who were not given sufficient backup or safety information by their male colleagues in the hope that they would fail, even die. I knew women fire fighters, army and navy officers, research physicians, assembly-line workers who were sexually harassed, even assaulted, on the job—then fired if they complained.

Where can a woman file her grievance? After all, Anita Hill was sexually harassed by her boss, Clarence Thomas, who was at that time the head of the Equal Employment Opportunities Commission and is now a sitting Supreme Court justice. I know professional women who were ordered into psychiatric treatment because they alleged sex discrimination. This was—and still is—epidemic; the persistence and courage of the women is nothing less than astounding.

You are entitled to know our war stories. We cannot, in good conscience, send you into battle without giving you a very clear idea of what may happen there.

Great women scientists, such as Barbara McClintock and Rita Levi-Montalcini, who both received Nobel Prizes, only did so when they were already in their seventies and eighties—although they'd been doing extraordinary work for nearly half a century. Marie Curie, the first woman to receive a Nobel Prize, was never admitted to the French Academie des Sciences. Great women must be twice as great and settle for a fraction of the rewards that great men come by sooner and more easily.

At least McClintock and Levi-Montalcini were eventually honored. The scientist Rosalind Franklin died very young of cancer. James Watson, Francis Crick, and Maurice Wilkins (of double helix fame) used Franklin's work without crediting her—work for which *they* received a Nobel Prize. I'd like to propose that Franklin receive posthumous recognition, but what should we do about the ignoble Watson, Crick, and Wilkins, who have enjoyed such honor for so many years?

Given how routinely truly great women have been dishonored, I've been lucky. I had a job and I kept it. I know many supremely accomplished women who were never hired as professors in the first place, whose contracts were not renewed, or who were only allowed to work as adjuncts for tiny sums of money without any security or benefits. I know brilliant, hardworking feminists whom universities undermined, overwhelmed, underpaid, harassed, and fired—long before economic recession/depression set in.

What I'm about to describe happened to many radical feminist women lucky enough to have held a university position in the last thirty years.

In 1969-70, I taught one of the first accredited women's studies courses and went on to co-found one of the first women's studies programs in the country. At the time, I was the only woman in my psychology department. Within a year, I had successfully lobbied my all-male colleagues to hire seven (super-qualified) women for ten available positions.

It didn't matter that, overall, women comprised more than 55 percent of the student body and less than 15 percent of the faculty. In my time, the acceptance of even *one* woman into a previously all-male space was enough. Two women? That's a takeover. Seven women? A bloody act of war. I didn't know this, no one warned me—but even if they had, I would have done the same thing, only I'd have been better prepared for battle, less amazed that my actions would provoke unending retaliation. The fact that I was, early on, also associated with the women's class-action lawsuit against our university didn't help. Every principled action I ever took hurt my academic career.

Know that you too may be punished for fighting back, whether you do so alone or with others. But know that if you persevere, you *may* improve the fate of future generations.

I loved teaching, I loved my students. I lectured with passion and devotion. I "hung out" with my students, invited them over for coffee, just as if they were at Oxford or Cambridge, and not at a working-class public institution. Those with power over me sometimes *accused* me of holding extra classes off-campus and verbally threatened me with exposure and expulsion for doing so.

By 1972, certain colleagues, administrators, and well-briefed students routinely began to bring charges against me: I was anti-male, I used "sexually explicit" language, I forced my students to read irrelevant feminist works, I didn't "love" my students enough (perhaps the way a Good Mother should). How could I? they reasoned, when I was lecturing, off-campus, on the airwaves, and publishing too!

These charges—and rumors about these charges—had a continuing life of their own during the course of my academic career. Nothing I ever accomplished had as much weight as the rumor that I'd once been accused (never tried, or convicted)—of something, whatever it was.

There we were—beginning to put a strong feminist agenda into place on *their* campuses; there *we* were—founding and attending women's caucuses within the professions, coordinating speak-outs, taking part in televised demonstrations, being quoted in the newspapers, presenting papers at academic conferences, teaching our students differently (better, I think). Each pioneer academic feminist was a local symbol of the national ferment. The patriarchal powers-that-be both feared and hated us, and acted accordingly.

For about ten years, radical feminists were very much in demand on college campuses, on television, in publishing, on legislative panels—but mainly as "dancing dogs." Most pioneer whistle-blowers did not, however, inherit the best academic perches. Those jobs went to ever-younger white men, and then to token numbers of non-radical or anti-feminist women and people of color.

In my case, it took twenty-two years before I was promoted to full professor. Male colleagues with far fewer publications to their credit often accomplished this in ten years. Over the years, those colleagues who kept voting against my promotions actually said, "But you're only publishing things about women! That doesn't count." Or, "You're publishing too much." It took more than twenty-eight years before I was allowed to teach graduate students at my own university.

John Demos, in *Entertaining Satan*, a study of the Salem witchcraft trials, points out that people—mainly, but not only, women—were arrested, tried, tortured, and killed as witches not because they *were* witches, but because the Inquisitors were able to get away with it; their victims were vulnerable.

Those accused of witchcraft hadn't really "entertained Satan," nor had the Jews been responsible for Germany's economic tragedy, nor had Moslem and Croatian Bosnians been preparing to destroy the Serbs, nor had the Tutsi in Rwanda been preparing to slaughter the Hutus. False propaganda has always been easily able to arouse barely suppressed hatreds; the rest is tragedy.

After more than thirty years of struggle, I, like many radical feminists, still have very little *institutional* power. Without it, what we know dies with us. Our books do not stay in print long enough to do that work for us; even when they do, they are usually taught only in women's studies classes. Feminist work is not often required reading for everyone. Most of us are not delivering commencement addresses or receiving honorary degrees.

Today, many students—including young feminists—are not familiar with the feminist classics of both the First and Second Waves. Some say that young people today are cynical, not interested in idealistic activism. I disagree—but unless their parents or older siblings were active feminists, they haven't had a chance—at least, not in school, and not in virtual patriarchal reality—to see feminists do these things, over and over again. Like breathing. That's a terrible loss. For me—and for you too.

Feminist work, even if it's bold and groundbreaking, just has a way of slipping through our collective fingers and down into a living death. I know feminist authors whose work has literally changed the world but who haven't been able to find a publisher for years; I know feminists whose *work* is being taught at the very universities that would never have hired them as professors. Within a decade, we saw some of our greatest feminist ideas distorted, then "disappeared." By the early 1980s, our best consciousness-raising pamphlets and street-corner speeches were forgotten, buried under mounds of reactionary media coverage and sometimes incomprehensible academic papers.

Even as I write, women—people—are dying and here I am, talking about feminist books going out of print! How dare I complain? These feminist visionaries are not dead—although some are; not homeless—although some are; not in jail—although some are. They may be unable to continue their feminist work, but at least they do not have to earn their living on their backs—although some do.

Ultimately, the women at my university won our class-action lawsuit. A judge agreed that the university discriminated against women, but the lawsuit took more than eighteen years, and the remedies were token at best. By the time the lawsuit settled, many of the women in the "class" had died, moved on, retired on shrunken pensions, gotten sick, given up. No one's lost years of productivity and status among their peers were restored.

I am not saying that class-action lawsuits are a waste of time. On the contrary. Recently, however, the federal government has made such suits even harder to bring. (They realize something about the power of collective action.) Without a class-action suit underway, I doubt that many of us could have borne the continued indignities and injustices at work. Without a lawsuit, one by one, we each would have been isolated, humiliated, threatened, fired. Had we tried to speak out as individuals, our allegations might have been brushed off as the misguided beliefs of a few crazy or difficult women. Had we not fought, the next generations of feminist scholars would never have gained even a toehold in the academy.

Fight like hell to transform your educational institutions. But you must also create your own programs, your own schools too. Even if your kitchen-table alternative schools don't last (few do), you'll be full of memories and wisdom, and you will have trained at least a generation or two.

As an academic woman, I was far luckier than women who began working in blue-collar—previously all-male—bastions of power: firefighters, police officers, electricians. As academics, we were (only) verbally intimidated, ostracized, not rewarded for our accomplishments. While some of us were sexually harassed, and re-victimized when we legally "grieved," few of us were physically beaten, firebombed, raped, purposefully exposed to physically dangerous situations by our colleagues as a way of getting us to flee the boys-only club.

The women miners in Eveleth, Minnesota, who worked at the Oglebey Norton company, were not as lucky. Beginning in 1975, these women were subjected to both a physically and sexually hostile work environment. In an ongoing class-action lawsuit, at least nineteen women miners charged repeated incidents of serious and intimidating harassment: a male co-worker had ejaculated into a woman's locker; a second male co-worker had exposed himself to another woman, then broke into her house and attempted to "embrace her"; a third man had knifed a woman in the leg; a fourth man had simulated choking a woman; a fifth man had physically menaced a woman with a giant dildo; a sixth man threatened to kill a woman whom he called "the little bitch," by "throwing her into the concentrator bins." (Indeed, she would have been ground to bits.) All the women were routinely stalked at home and on the job, referred to as "dogs," subjected to sexual graffiti. Posted outside the personnel director's office was a sign: "Sexual Harassment Will Not Be Reported. However, It Will Be Graded." The union refused to intervene. The women sued.

It took years for the women to establish their right to sue as a class (a precedent decision which has already been used by other women), years before Oglebey Norton was found liable for damages. Then, the Eveleth women were themselves put on trial. Their psychological and gynecological records, including information about past abortions and rapes, were entered into evidence. In the course of this lawsuit, the women have been ostracized by their neighbors. To date, one woman has died, and four women have dropped out. Perhaps the stress of being put on trial was too much to endure.

In 1996, more than twenty years after their ordeal first began, a judge awarded the women miners monetary damages so minimal that they have appealed the decision.

You may not be planning to be a miner. You may already be studying to be a lawyer, a stockbroker, a veterinarian, a pilot. Nevertheless, it is important to remember that what happened in Eveleth is what women are still subjected to in America when they try to earn enough money to support themselves and their families.

Submission and humility will not protect you from the injustices of this war. Nothing can. But clarity, and solidarity in action, will allow you to fight back—and to keep sane, no matter what happens.

I was incredibly naive when I was younger. I thought I should be offered a place of honor at the patriarchal table—for my feminist work. I was foolish, but human, for wanting that. It took me time to understand that women—myself included—would remain oppressed for a long time, no matter how fast any individual woman could dance and shine. As Aristotle once wrote: "Revolutions may also arise when persons of great ability, and second to none in their merits, are treated dishonorably by those who themselves enjoy the highest honors."

He was right.

Do not try to win approval from your opponents. Merely fight to win.

While it is important to stand your ground, it is dangerous to get accustomed to standing on it in just one way. I am so used to being opposed that, to this day, I am still surprised, even discomfited, when too many others agree with me. "Have I lost it?" I ask myself, each time. Recently, a young journalist interviewed me. In the midst of my answering his questions, he paused, very sweetly came closer, touched my arm and said, simply, "Phyllis, we're with you. You don't have to make the case from scratch. We're with you."

Feminist Myths about Sisterhood

YOU CAN NEITHER STAND YOUR GROUND nor forge ahead without feminist friends and comrades.

Cherish those you have. And choose wisely, if you can. People tend to uphold a family-like loyalty to friends—even when they're virulent misogynists. Feminists do this too.

The feminists in my generation empowered each other in ways that nothing else ever did or could. Together, joyfully, we participated in a quantum leap forward in consciousness. Many of us believed our own ecstatic rhetoric: that we were "sisters." I certainly believed this. We understood how important women were to each other in terms of emotional intimacy. We also began to understand that we'd need to encourage boldness and rebelliousness in other women—partly by becoming like that ourselves.

We sometimes succeeded at this; more often, we failed.

This task remains.

I expected so much of other feminists—we all did—that the most ordinary disappointments were often experienced as major betrayals. We expected less of men and forgave them, more than once, when they failed us. We expected far more of other women, who, paradoxically, had less (power) to share than men did. We held grudges against other women in ways we dared not do against men. We were not always aware of this.

Be aware of such unspoken double standards. Try and behave more evenhandedly than we did.

As feminist women, we knew we were doomed without sisterhood so we proclaimed it, even in its absence. We wanted to will it into existence, verbally, without wrestling it into being. We didn't understand that the sisterhood we so eagerly proclaimed was, like brotherhood, only an ideal, not yet a reality, that we'd have to create sisterhood, daily, against considerable odds.

As individuals, most women I knew were unable to "love our sisters as we loved ourselves." We didn't love ourselves enough.

This was true for anti-feminist women too.

It is a myth that women are more "peaceful" or "compassionate" than men are. Women, like men, are hard on women. *Like everyone else* the feminists of my generation did not automatically trust or respect women. We thought we should. We said we did. However, our need to pretend to ourselves that we were less woman-hating than the rest of the human race was unfortunate.

Franz Fanon and James Baldwin have written about skin-color prejudice among colonized Africans and African-Americans; Albert Memmi and Primo Levi have written about anti-Semitism among Jews. My feminist generation was eerily silent about woman-hating among women, including among feminists.

In 1980, when I first told friends that I had begun to interview women on this very subject, most of them were disapproving. One feminist leader told me that "some of my best friends were women." (Yes, she actually said that.) Another leader said that "I've had a very good relationship with my mother so what you are saying can't be true." A third leader said that "men will use this against us so you'd better not publish anything." A fourth asked, worriedly, "Are you going to name names?"

"Name names? I might as well publish the telephone book annually," I'd responded.

Within a decade—it took that long—these same feminists all asked me, repeatedly, where that study of mine was, that they/we needed it.

My feminist generation psychologically arose one morning, or so it seemed, right out of the primordial "frontlash." Like the goddess Athena, newly hatched from her father Zeus's brow, we, too, wanted to experience ourselves as motherless "daughters."

We were a sibling horde of "sisters." Although we were many different ages, psychologically, we lived in a universe of same-age peers. We knew of no other way to break with the past. There were no living "mothers" moving among us. Of course, in real life, some of us *were* mothers, some of us even loved our real mothers, but when we stepped out onto the stage of history we did so primarily as motherless daughters/sisters/sibling rivals.

Psychologically, we had committed matricide—the equivalent of what Freud said that sons do to fathers. Of course, Freud had it wrong, it's the other way round: fathers "kill" sons, despite which sons still continue to hunger for their fathers' love and to scapegoat their mothers for its absence.

Most feminist daughters did not notice what we'd done, or why. Many of us rather hotly denied that this was so. To this day, some of the most brilliant voices of my feminist generation continue to speak in the voice of The Daughter Risen, and not that of The Mother-Teacher.

Behind closed doors, we behaved towards women the way most women did: we envied, competed with, feared, and were ambivalent about other women; we also loved and needed them. My feminist generation ate our leaders. Some feminists who were really good at this became our leaders.

I saw feminists do the same things to each other that anti-feminists did: seduce each others' boyfriends or girlfriends, endlessly confront each other, or, more maddeningly, refuse to say anything directly, wreck each others' reputations, never acknowledge doing so, turn personal rivalries into "political" issues that demanded that everyone choose sides or become automatically seen as the enemy of both sides.

Typical sorority—hardly revolutionary—behavior. Over and over again, feminists would choose one woman (not one principle) over another, and, once they did, they often failed to hold their chosen sister to any ethical or political standards. If your sister plagiarizes the works of others—so what? If she tells lies—who's counting? If she commits immoral and illegal acts—doesn't sisterhood demand a cover-up?

I saw feminists steal each others' work, money, jobs, spouses, physically hit each other, padlock doors, turn other feminists in to the police. I saw feminists either refuse to pay or grossly underpay their female employees, or "groupies," whom they sometimes also treated as if they were stupid, slaves, or servants. I knew of feminist therapists who routinely had sex with their patients—I took a principled stand against this, but it often took others years to do so. I saw feminists instigate whisper-and-smear campaigns to wreck each others' reputations, both socially and professionally. Often, the women had once loved and admired each other. Eventually, one by one, a feminist who was well-known in her own circle would simply disappear—or so it seemed. More often, what had happened was she'd been dropped from the guest lists—and never told why. Perhaps someone thought she was too pretty, too angry, not the right color, or class, too outspoken, unpredictable; perhaps she slept with the wrong people, refused to sleep with the right person, or had chosen the wrong side.

Our male patriarchal adversaries used brute force and guns to wipe their competitors out. Feminists sometimes accomplished this psychologically, with words only.

As much as we longed for sisterhood, we only started the process; we failed at the task.

Feminists are not unique; this behavior is typical of any oppressed group. Therefore, you must act generously—not enviously. Learn to respect other feminists: both those who bring great light, and those who are warmed by it. Do not ostracize the woman who refuses to bend to a party line, or the woman who is willing to die for one. Remember: It is amazing that women are fighting back at all; we are not meant to. Respect other feminists, but don't worship them. Learn to recognize what a cult is and how to avoid it.

For example, some of us revered, rather than became, the women we most admired. Sometimes we found ourselves drawn to a feminist who was quite abusive to women. We believed in her work and wished to bask in the light of her fame or ideas; as women, we were used to glory via association. Perhaps we also hoped that if we loved and served The Great Woman well and long enough, that she'd turn into the kind of mother/sister/ daughter we longed to have.

If not, we'd just pretend she had, or we'd make her pay in other ways. (Groupies always get even.) Always, we'd use our association with her to keep other women in awe of us.

Try not to repeat this mistake. By all means, learn from a mentor, assist her, but do not think you can live through her. Doing so is of little use. Do not assume that what she can do, with your help, is also yours. It is—but it isn't. And if she doesn't treat you respectfully—walk away.

It is dangerous to revere someone who abuses you, foolish to believe that such abuse is your contribution to the cause. Beware of drowning in others, whether they are men or women, even if they are charismatic and brilliant. Access to a great leader is not as important as *becoming* a great leader.

While I encourage you to become a leader in at least one area, let me be clear: there is no shame in being part of a team. A feminist must learn to do both. Not one or the other: both.

Feminists who commit psychological matricide and feminists who form cults are not mutually exclusive phenomena. The same feminists who formed cults around needy, damaged women were also quite capable of destroying less needy, less damaged women. Women in groups often try to destroy spontaneity and strength in women; men in groups try to destroy the man who is seen as weak.

Strength in a woman can include advanced educational skills—or street smarts; too much money—or no money at all; a personal style that is too expressive—or one that is too cautious, withholding. Generosity is a strength. The daughter in us all often treats a well-endowed, generous woman as a natural resource. We use her like we use the Earth itself, and when the well runs dry, we discard it and move on in search of another.

The way mothers are often discarded. The way I discarded mine.

Beware of one of my generation's most mistaken assumptions: namely, that no special skills are required in order to accomplish a great task.

There are—and you must develop those skills in order to accomplish yours. However, not everyone can—or needs to—develop the same skills.

Like other powerless groups, my generation of feminists found it easier to *verbally* confront and humiliate another feminist than to *physically* confront patriarchal power in male form.

As women, we had been taught that women were responsible for controlling or appeasing violent men and for maintaining family peace and connectedness. Thus, many women were uncomfortable when they disconnected—even from their batterers. As women, we had been trained to fight male intimates indirectly, privately, verbally. We had not been taught to fight publicly and directly *against* a male intimate—one of many reasons we usually lost everything in divorce and custody battles.

As women, we had not been trained to fight male non-intimates publicly. It was gender-appropriate to fight only with other women, or with children, not with men.

Just because we were feminists didn't mean we had gotten beyond the gender code.

We called each other "sisters." Thus, we had no vocabulary for the things that happened between women, quite apart from our real *political* differences. Resentments built, then exploded into take-no-prisoner emotional showdowns. Eventually, feminists did begin to confront each other about our racism, homophobia, anti-Semitism, even classism—a real American unmentionable. Blood boiled, tempers flared, hearts broke. And then, we often never spoke again. There was no safe space to talk about what we were doing to each other.

Please remember to always create safe spaces to discuss how feminists also internalize patriarchy.

Doing feminist work is not a way of getting your every psychological or economic need met. Movements cannot flourish if their members are there mainly for therapeutic or career reasons. You have a responsibility to see that your wounded selves do not get in the way of your warrior selves.

Therefore, it is important to neither minimize nor deny the facts and consequences of oppression. Some feminists of my generation did just this: insist that the "enemy" was primarily "out there," never within. But we also had plenty of self-involved navel gazers, who denied all political reality and insisted that if they, personally, "felt" free, we were *all* free.

What I want you to remember is this: Oppression is real. It works. Torture, especially sexual torture, demoralizes, cripples, and induces self-hatred and self-destructiveness. Being traumatized does not necessarily, in and of itself, make one a noble or productive person. Some rise above it; others don't. Some victims of rape and battery want feminist support and advice; others don't. Some women want to save themselves; others are too damaged to participate in their own redemption.

In my day, I saw many a good feminist also act out: some saw enemies everywhere, even when they weren't there; some acted as if they were God's personal prophets; some experienced themselves as "helpless" victims, rather than as avenging dominatrixes. We're flawed, human, just like anti-feminists are. It is important to understand that otherwise extraordinary leaders and comrades can *also* be extremely fragile, limited, wounded, mad, evil, over-bearing, over-sensitive—simply too interpersonally challenged to work with or befriend.

Therefore, one must try not to confuse their behavior with their inspiring ideas.

If you yourself have been traumatized, it is crucial that you tell those whom you trust or with whom you work what your vulnerabilities and limitations are. There is no shame in saying that you are unable to attend a meeting if you have to return home late at night alone, or that you don't take elevators, or that you are afraid of bridges and tunnels, suffer panic attacks, etc. You don't necessarily need to share the reasons: you were raped, you're a battered woman, the child of alcoholic parents, an accident victim. It is better to spell out what you need in order to do the work than to end up sounding like this: "I won't be on this committee if you don't always meet at my apartment (or at my friend's nearby apartment)."

It is crucial that you acknowledge your psychological problem areas—at least to yourself. Try not to humiliate, exploit, badmouth, alienate others because you, too, are hurting. Act *in spite* of it, try not to use the fact of your abuse as explanation or justification for why you (unconsciously) hurt others.

You will make terrible mistakes. Acknowledge them. Leaders will disappoint you. Expect this.

A leader is not always a mentor; a mentor is not a faery goddess-mother in charge of an "old girls network." We don't have an "old girls network," not yet. You must know this, and not assume that one exists that is kept hidden from you. What we have is hard work which we must do *together.* Sometimes a woman who is married to the right man, or born to the right family, may choose to use her access to benefit a protégé or a cause. This is fine. It is not an "old girls network."

Young feminists often talk about mentors as if one can't proceed without them.

You can. We did.

In my view, a mentor is neither an all-giving mother or a feel-good goddess. She is not the final authority, you are not the lowly peon. What you bring to her (or him) is also crucial. Reciprocity is everything.

Also, please remember: a pioneer is someone who breaks with the past. She is not easy to mentor—nor should she be—for she does not automatically obey authority. A mentor is more mother than friend, but more midwife than mother.

Self-Love and Team-Spirit

THE MOST RADICAL FEMINISTS of my generation were not always
kind or even minimally civilized towards each other. In our rush
towards freedom, we threw off as much "femininity" as we
could. We had no time to make small talk; we needed all our
available time for work. This meant that, unless we were
independently wealthy and had a staff (some did), we no longer
cooked for others, or spent too much time "listening" to them
either. Sometimes even the simple niceties—like introducing
women to each other or saying thank you—were far beyond (or
behind) us.

We were arrogant and obsessed, we had to be, but such
behavior is unacceptable over the long haul where decency and
kindness matter.

Am I saying that women should never raise their voices,
not even in the heat of battle? No, I am not.

I don't want a "nice" girl (or boy) covering my back in battle—I want someone who can get the job done. In battle, people do yell, curse, insult each other.

You must find ways to disagree with each other without annihilating each other, ways to move on. As a feminist, you need to figure out how to encourage, not destroy, your comrades. Men follow sports- and business-based rules for this. Women usually don't.

While men are the number one killers of other men, paradoxically, men are also geniuses at buddying up. One reason for this may involve their extensive early experience in bonding through team sports, either as players or avid spectators.

In the past and, in my view, still today, most women are used to only *one* woman among many winning a competition: there is only *one* Miss America, one wife at a time, one Homecoming Queen. Men—and those women who participate in team sports that have been traditionally considered male-only sports—are used to experiencing individual victory as part of a group effort. Thus, more men than women are psychologically primed to compete against others of their own gender as part of a team. Often, whether they win or lose, male athletes quickly let go of their competitive edge, enjoy drinks with the victors and losers, live to play another day.

More often, women socialized as "women" tend to hold grudges, or refuse to play again if it means they might lose. More often, women do not choose the strongest woman to be on their "sorority" team; they do not understand that her strength will work for—not against—them. (Men will often bypass the weakest men for this same reason.) Unlike women, men can often walk away at the end of the day without having their self-esteem, their very identities, undermined by what happened at work.

Women athletes often develop certain kinds of psychological characteristics.

Women who are involved in competive team sports, especially at a young age, learn that you can't win alone; that, in fact, you have to become assertive, even aggressive, both for your own sake and for the sake of a team. Women learn that competing head-on for the gold is desirable; that if you lose one day, you won't die, it's not all over, you may very well win the next day; that falling down, getting bruised, getting dirty, won't kill you.

Women in locker rooms also learn that women's bodies vary, and that all kinds of bodies are beautiful. In fact, becoming physically strong, feeling your body's power, can translate into strength and confidence in other areas of your life. Becoming physically strong is not enough. Gymnasts and ballet dancers are strong but they often suffer from eating disorders. Some studies suggest that team players are the athletes who suffer less often from eating disorders than non-team players do. More important, studies suggest that both female and male athletes are highly affiliative and are less stressed and frustrated when faced with the need to make quick decisions.

Some other athletic "virtues" women should apply elsewhere in their lives:

- how to jockey for the ball, not merely for attention;
- how to experience one's body as strong and capable of both aggression and resistance;
- how to work as a team towards a common goal;

- how the needs of the whole team supersede—without negating—the needs of the individual athlete;
- how to feel part of something larger than one's self, or than one's self merged with only one other;
- how to enjoy a non-sexual union with other sweaty bodies, set free from the ordinary, everyday barriers that separate us from one another;
- how to enjoy one's body for what it does rather than for how it looks.

It is important to respect your sister as you respect yourself. You don't have to love her, or even like her. You don't have to be like her either.

Our strength is in diversity, not uniformity. It's important to cut the next woman some slack, give her the benefit of the doubt until she proves you wrong in a major way and more than once. Even then, if you have a battle to wage in common, you may still have to find a way to work together.

In order to do this, we have to respect and love ourselves a great deal.

If we are not strong, our offers of help are minimally useful. If we are not strong enough to take care of ourselves—no one else can really help us. For example, it is up to each feminist to stop the violence against women and children. I am not suggesting illegal, vigilante revenge squads. I am suggesting that feminists begin to understand—really understand—that no one will rescue women and children from violence but us. And we don't know how to do that. And we'd better start thinking about it.

Given how prevalent rape is, in both war and peace, why do we resist teaching women how to think strategically about defending themselves?

Thus, I implore you to enroll your young daughters as well as your sons in competitive team sports—not against their wills, only if they seem to like it; not primarily for your sake, but for their sakes alone.

Enroll your young daughters in self-defense classes at an early age.

Enroll yourself, at any age, in what I call Warrior Training 101. It's never too late.

Principles, Not Popularity

I AM NOT DRAWN to an individual woman's plight, or case, because that woman is my friend, or because she and I are so much alike. Acting in the service of one's principles is not the same as acting on behalf of one's family and friends; the rewards are different. They are not the traditional (female) rewards of being liked or popular. The rewards are impersonal and eternal; they resound forever.

If you find yourself opposed (or not strongly supported) by groups who usually oppose each other—you're probably doing radical feminist work. Know that you will be criticized by your own people. You must learn not to let that stop you. For example, in 1987, I got involved in the Baby M surrogacy-custody battle. Many liberals, both feminists and patriarchs, did not view Mary Beth Whitehead, Baby M's birth mother, as an appropriate hero.

Mary Beth was a stay-at-home working-class mother. She had no high-status career; her husband, a Vietnam veteran, was a sanitation worker. To some, this made them less preferable parents than Bill Stern, Ph.D., the sperm-donor, and his wife, Betsy Stern, M.D. In my view, if Mary Beth's right to refuse to surrender her surrogate-contract daughter for adoption was violated, so might those of other women.

Mary Beth Whitehead was amazed that *feminists* had come out to demonstrate on her behalf. That king of journalism, the late, great, Murray Kempton, actually came over to shake my hand. "You are an utterly unexpected sight," said he.

Many feminists did not support Norma Jean McCorvey (the "Roe" of *Roe v. Wade*). Or Lorena Bobbitt, who cut her batterer's penis off. Or Ellie Nesler, who shot her son's sexual abuser to death in court. These women were not feminists. Their class, level of anger, neediness, or vigilante action-readiness made them unsuitable as perfect victims. They were not ladies. Some feminists sometimes criticized me for supporting these women; they perceived this as endangering our fight for the rights of more deserving, "nicer" women.

You will sometimes be supported, unexpectedly, by an anti-feminist group. Remain true to your own principles, set limits beyond which you will not go—but work with these occasional allies. For example, some concerned Catholics joined our picket line outside the Baby M courthouse. I had no problem *demonstrating* with these people of good will. However, I refused to work with legislators and crusaders who wanted to criminalize surrogacy because these were the same legislators who wanted to criminalize abortion. I did not want to give them any mileage. Some feminists chose to work with them, even though it was clear that these crusaders sought to exploit the feminist sensation over surrogacy for their own non-feminist fund-raising purposes.

We were all good feminists. We did not—nor did we—have to agree on everything. Too often, people withdraw, then mount dangerous crusades against each other for holding different views, or for being "different" in other ways. Know that you can disagree with someone without having to hate or banish them. This is an important moral and political skill to learn.

In 1991, I became involved in a very different kind of case, that of Aileen Carol Wuornos, referred to as "the world's first female serial killer," a prostituted woman accused of killing at least six johns. Wuornos was also surprised that other women, especially feminists, were interested in her case.

What interested me was the issue of a woman's right to self-defense, including her right to kill her rapist. Again, some feminists thought that Wuornos was guilty anyway, and too crazy to bother with. Understandably, they feared that supporting a completely unsympathetic woman might weaken support for "nice" girls who, after suffering for a long time, had killed (only) one batterer. I thought it was time to expand the battered woman's defense to include prostituted women. I thought Wuornos was entitled to a fair trial. Of course, she did not get one.

Wuornos is a "bad" girl. However, even very "good" girls are viewed as brazen revolutionaries when they demand to be treated as human beings, even when they define their humanity as (only) a "separate but equal" place at their Father's Table.

I took what European intellectuals said seriously: it's important to put your body where your ideas are. For example, since 1988, I have been involved in an historic battle for women's religious rights in Jerusalem. On December 1, 1988, I was one of seventy Jewish women who prayed together, in the women-only section, in a group, out loud, with a Torah, wearing ritual garments, at the Kotel (or Western Wall) in Jerusalem—the holiest place in the world to Jews. What we did at the Wall in 1988 was, in a sense, analogous to nuns taking over the Vatican and helping at mass. What we did was historic—uncustomary, but absolutely permissible according to Jewish law.

On the men's side, dozens, maybe hundreds, of Torah scrolls and prayer books reside. A variety of religious quorums take place among the men three times a day. On the women's side, there is no Torah, no religious quorums, no group spirit, no solidarity. Only solitary, eerily silent women, sometimes weeping, some-times clutching a prayer book, silently mouthing their prayers.

When we prayed, other worshippers, both men and women, verbally and physically assaulted us. We asked the Israeli state to maintain public order so that we could exercise our religious and civil rights. The state claimed it could not contain the violence against us, and that we ourselves had provoked the violence by "disturbing or offending" the "sensi-bilities of Jews at worship."

Some secular feminists took us to task for "caring about a symbol of a patriarchal empire." "Who wants a piece of that tainted pie? If you absolutely must 'do' religion, why not found a Goddess grove, embrace Buddhism, open a soup kitchen?" Our feminist detractors were united in the belief that we were asking for too little and the wrong thing.

The fundamentalist right was not lulled by the fact that some *feminists* seemed to oppose us. In their brief, the Israeli state and Ministry of Religion referred to Women of the Wall and our international committee as "witches," who were doing "Satan's work"; "more like prostitutes than holy women"; "misled, tainted, by modern secular feminism."

It is crucial to fight for territory. In this case, the territory is real, but it is also psychological and spiritual. In my view, grand vision, coupled with human, imperfect action is everything. If we wait for the exact right moment to do the most politically correct action in the company of the most politically correct people . . . don't hold your breath, it will never happen. Without ground troops in action, you've got nothing.

Victory is quiet, more humdrum than dramatic. Victory consists of former slaves, or second-class citizens, engaging in ordinary activities, taking their right to do so for granted. They live, instead of dying. They attend school, find employment, vote, have an abortion, exercise their right to prayerfully greet their newborn, bury their dead, have a Bat Mitzvah at the Kotel.

Not every pioneer will personally benefit from the particular wrong righted, the right won. Not everyone who begins a battle may be able to see it through to the end. Perhaps others, especially the coming generations, will be the ones to most benefit from our struggle.

On March 6, 1996, while all Israel reeled from the four terrorist bomb attacks in Jerusalem and Tel Aviv, Women of the Wall went to the Kotel to read the story of how Queen Esther saved the Jews of Persia. No one said, "Oh, it's the wrong time, there are more important things to worry about." No one hesitated or had the slightest doubt about the importance of what they were doing or worried about what others might think.

For women, this is often the first, and most important, battle to win.

In November of 1996, our praying women were again physically attacked. The police did not silence the verbally riotous men, nor did they arrest those who were throwing wooden objects and hurling insults at our women. Instead, ten police officers pushed eighty women at prayer back one hundred feet.

Amidst the chaos and pandemonium, our women did not stop praying.

Remember Ruth Orkin's photo of street harassment in Italy? Orkin's young woman is no longer alone. Feminists are with her, facing a greater number of staring, angry men. In my view, we are just beginning to hold our own.

As are Brenda and Wanda Henson, the founders of Camp Sister Spirit, a 120-acre feminist education retreat in Ovett, Mississippi. The Hensons have not dropped out, nor have they sold out. In the face of violent attacks, they and their many male and female volunteer supporters are maintaining a level of visibility and virtue that is almost pure science fiction.

Camp Sister Spirit has been under siege since 1993. The Hensons and their supporters have become high-profile symbols of feminist resistance. The Hensons are feminists who are lesbians. They are out of the closet but their political principles and actions define them as truly as does their sexual preference.

Some citizens of Ovett were so outraged that feminist lesbians had dared to buy land in their neighborhood that they simply started shooting at women at point-blank range. Shots were fired at the Hensons' front gate. Roofing tacks were placed on their roads. Their American and rainbow flags were repeatedly torn down. Intruders kept appearing on their property. Low-flying planes took photos. The camp received threatening phone calls, letters, and bomb threats. Two sanitary napkins and a dead female puppy were draped across their mailbox. A local lesbian supporter's house mysteriously burned down. A caller warned, "Expect the KKK to burn a cross on you."

I first went to Ovett on Memorial Day weekend in 1994, in response to a call for solidarity.

The moon was out, I was enchanted by the sultry southern night air. Camp Sister Spirit was like Woodstock, Lesbian Nation, and the Michigan Women's Music Festival, but it was also like Mississippi Freedom Summer, the Mothers of the Plaza de Mayo, a Goddess grove, and a Girl Scout camp. Ah, it was like nothing else. It's as if Diana Rivers's tale about a tribe of psychic-military lesbian feminist warriors (*Daughters of the Great Star*) had come to life, and there I was, sitting with them. Magically, Rivers herself was there, too.

Camp Sister Spirit is not a young, butch paramilitary encampment. True, there are swaggers, buzz cuts, muscles, and bared breasts galore, but there are women in skirts and jewelry here too, women in their fifties and sixties, mothers and grandmothers with gray hair and smiling wrinkles. No one has come here to die. They are here to support the kind of grassroots work with rape and incest victims, battered women and children, that feminists have been doing for years.

We're so naive, so American, that we don't really believe we can be killed for our beliefs. Not here in the land of the free, the home of the brave.

Camp Sister Spirit is utterly sober: chemically, psychologically, and politically. The women are security-conscious—they have to be. Like nuns, they patrol the property in pairs and communicate with walkie-talkies. The women of Camp Sister Spirit have been forced, very much against their wills, to build a fence around the property. ("We could have fed a hundred families for ten years with the money the fence is costing us," Wanda Henson says.) The women are legally armed. Everyone keeps track of where everyone else is.

It's scary, isn't it, when women really start loving themselves enough to draw boundaries and defend their bodies and minds from attack.

Questions abound. Why should the feminist-government-in-exile choose Jones County, the historical heart of the Ku Klux Klan, as its first outpost on earth? "Why *not* in Mississippi—the poorest state in the nation, and the most oppressed," Wanda says. "It's where I was born, it's where I'm from." And where exactly are radical lesbian feminists wanted anyway?

Some ask, Why is the camp courting such danger? Why not retreat to some safer place? That would be nice, but women are always in danger—in our homes, at work, on hiking trails. Refusing to become conscious about one's oppression doesn't make you safe; it just keeps you in denial. At Camp Sister Spirit, the women are very conscious of danger: their own, and all women's everywhere. They've chosen to face the danger together, collectively. At Camp Sister Spirit no death will go unmourned or misunderstood.

Equally fearless, and dedicated, Canadian feminists have been working on the Women's Memorial Monument Project— arguably the first of its kind in the world. This is unbelievable, but not surprising. In parks, at the entrance of public buildings, in museums, in town squares, one can see ten-to-twenty-feet-high statues of men on horseback, in uniform, holding flags, swords, guns, with their names, ranks, and deeds inscribed for all posterity. How few statues of women exist, how often they are half-naked, anonymous embodiments of Justice or Beauty.

The world has drowned, many times over, in hot seas of female blood. We do not know the names of the dead women, what they looked like, how they died, what they lived for, how they fought. This monument is the first to honor our unarmed soldiers, shot dead in one particular battle of a war that women never declared.

On December 6, 1989, Marc Lepine, a twenty-five-year-old Canadian armed with a semi-automatic rifle, entered the L'Ecole Polytechnique, an engineering school in Montreal. He ordered the men and women to stand at separate ends of the room. The students thought it was a joke until he fired a shot into the ceiling. Then he told the men to leave and started shouting at the women, "I want the women! You are all a bunch of fucking feminists. I hate feminists. Why should women be engineers and not men? You don't belong here." One student yelled back, "No, it's not true, we're not feminists." She was shot and killed anyway, along with thirteen other female students—simply because they were women. The killer injured thirteen others, nine women and five men.

The Montreal police insisted that this was the work of an isolated, deranged individual. However, in a letter written before the attack, Lepine described what he was about to do as a "political act aimed at women." He had a hit list of well-known feminists in his pocket. The day after the massacre, local university women's groups organized a vigil at the University of Montreal. At the last minute, some male students, who had agreed the night before to support the vigil, refused to provide the promised sound equipment. Some male students from the Polytechnique, using walkie-talkies, encircled the organizers and prevented them from speaking to the press or the crowd. These same men charged the organizers with "exploiting" the killing; they ordered the 5,000 Canadians who were waiting in sub-zero temperatures to disperse and go to a nearby church for silent prayer. Some men kept shouting that "speaking about the crime was disrespectful to the dead"; one man told the crowd that the "massacre was not to be interpreted as a gender issue." One feminist who tried to speak was drowned out by boos and catcalls. A physical scuffle broke out for control of the megaphone. National and local media reported that "feminists had tried to appropriate the vigil and had kept the men from grieving or speaking."

At the moment of the massacre, the male Polytechnique students mainly dove for cover—so much for counting on chivalry. And why should a male civilian take a bullet meant for someone else? However on August 20, 1990, eight months afterwards, Sarto Blais, a Polytechnique graduate who had been at the school during the massacre, killed himself. In a note, he wrote that "he could not accept that as a man he had been there and hadn't done anything about it." The head of security at the Polytechnique then said that "All the men who were present are bearing, in their minds, that responsibility."

This too is a sexist notion. Men are no more responsible than are women for not having stopped the massacre.

This massacre and its aftermath inspired the Memorial Monument as a "symbol of remembrance and call for change." Feminist volunteers and the Capilano College Women's Centre in Vancouver sponsored the project. A park in Vancouver was

donated to house artist Beth Alber's winning contribution—
fourteen benches of pink Quebec granite arranged in a three-
hundred-foot circle. Each bench will bear the name of one of the
women murdered at the L'Ecole Polytechnique.

Organizer Chris MacDowell says, "It is the women who are
murdered whom we must remember, not their killers. We
realized that so many women had been murdered that day, we
were unable to remember their names, but we couldn't forget the
name of their murderer." The inscription, in ten languages and
in Braille, will list the fourteen women's names after which it
will read: "We, their sisters and brothers, remember, and work
for a better world. In memory and in grief for all the women who
have been murdered by men. For women of all countries, all
classes, all ages, all colors."

Some people insist that feminists focus only on survivors
and forget or refuse to identify with victims. I say, we must focus
on both, of course; but only if we have the courage to face and
make visible that which shames and terrifies us, can we ever
begin the work of fighting back against the violence.

The Canadian monument feminists have been publicly
attacked for daring to say that it was a man (as opposed to what,
an alien?) who killed the fourteen women or that men (as
opposed to aliens, or bats, perhaps) are ever responsible for the
deaths of women. The monument feminists began distributing
fact sheets about the daily atrocities: "98 percent of women
murdered in Ontario between 1974 and 1990 were killed by
men, usually by an intimate partner. In 1991, 225 women were
murdered in Canada; of them, 208 were killed by a male family
member or acquaintance. A woman is hit by her husband or
partner an average of thirty times before she calls the police."

Men are victims of male violence too. Men often fight back. Those who do rarely feel that they are man-haters, nor do they often feel personally implicated because someone of their own gender is a woman-hater. (Sarto Blais may have been an exception.) Men who fight back are rarely attacked as man-haters. Only women are; only women fall for this.

If you are called a man-hater, do not deny it. Do not stop what you're doing in order to persuade your adversary that you are really a man-lover and a "nice" woman too. In feminist terms, "nice" means obedient to the patriarchal status quo. Is that *your* definition of "nice"? Is that how you want to be remembered?

I say, learn to enjoy the accusation of being a man-hater (or a man-hating dyke or whore). Do not take it personally. It is a poisoned insult, meant to paralyze you and fill you with self-doubt. This epithet, and much more, is the least of what can happen if you dare to fight back, even if only in your own small way, in your daily, personal life. One year after the massacre, in a speech at the University of Montreal, Andrea Dworkin said, "I think that the way we can honor these women who were executed for crimes they may or may not have committed—which is to say political crimes—is to commit every crime for which they were executed. . . . Each and every one of us has the responsibility to be the women that Marc Lepine wanted to murder."

Strong words, and true.

Susan B. Anthony's opponents burned a schoolhouse down after she spoke on behalf of female suffrage and against wife-abuse.

Once upon a time not so long ago in the mid eighties, a group of feminists decided to stop traffic with their bodies and hand out leaflets to midday motorists about how often women's lives in Massachusetts are ended by male violence. The police soon broke up the demonstration. They handcuffed and arrested Sandi Goodman, the ringleader, stashed her in the squad car, turned the key in the ignition, and attempted to head on out.

And then a small miracle occurred: the demonstrators surrounded the police car and would not let them leave with Sandi. The fear of being arrested, fined, even shot, did not stop these feminists from putting their bodies where their mouths were.

Endless discussion ensued but the police were forced to hand Sandi over to her jubilant comrades and leave without her.

A first—but, I hope, not the last event of its kind.

We Need a Feminist Continent

IN ONLY THIRTY YEARS, a visionary feminism has managed to seriously challenge, if not transform, world consciousness. Nevertheless, I am saddened and sobered by the realization that no more than a handful have been liberated from the lives of grinding poverty, illness, overwork, and endless worry that continues to afflict most people in the world.

My generation of feminists hit the ground running. We had a sense of collective destiny and invulnerability that now seems naive—and extraordinarily privileged. For the first time in our lives, we—and our analysis of reality—became the center of our universe. Feminists had (psychologically) declared that Man as woman's God on earth was dead—easily the equivalent of men's earlier secular, scientific, Marxist, and existential declarations that God and king were dead. Despite our considerable training as "Daddy's girls," we married History and each other. We wanted revolutionary transcendence, and justice, more than we wanted romantic love, or careers. Actually, we were Americans, and we wanted it all, but we'd been hungry for sisterhood in the service of *heroism* all our lives, without knowing it.

Some of us found more—and some found less—sisterhood and brotherhood than we'd dreamed possible, and for a while, we lived extraordinary lives. We did not transform the world— although it is a different world today than when we first started out. We had to fight for every inch of consciousness and dignity; the fight continues. Despite our willingness to make enormous sacrifices, many of us were still silenced, our work "disappeared" or watered down, our collective resistance rendered invisible, our ability to teach the next generations savagely curtailed.

Early on, I began talking about a feminist government in exile. How else, I asked, could we airlift women and children out of Bangladesh or Bosnia or Boston, i.e., out of patriarchy? For a long time now, and like many others, I've been a minister without portfolio, representing that future government.

What did my generation accomplish?

We pried open the imagination of the world, we opened ourselves to the cries of women in torment and to their yearnings for freedom and joy. We demanded justice for women. We wanted high-powered careers in formerly male-only pre-serves—*and* babies *and* sexual freedom—*and* political power. We expanded the boundaries of what women could want.

This was not our only important contribution.

Because of our work, the world now understands that wars do not only happen to male soldiers in uniform in foreign, enemy countries; they also happen at home, in the family, in times of so-called peace, to unarmed women and children. A 1997 New York City study—the first of its kind in the country—showed that 78 percent of women who were murdered were killed by husbands, boyfriends, relatives, or acquaintances. Of the 49 percent who were killed by husbands or boyfriends, one-third were killed when they tried to leave.

Because of our work, the world understands that women are endangered, not only by men, but by other women too. It is the women of the tribe who, in Mary Daly's phrase, are the "token torturers" of other women. It is women who genitally mutilate their daughters, women who banish their incestuously abused daughters—and not their abusive husbands, mother-in-laws who beat or help burn their daughters-in-law to death for dowry money. It is often women, worldwide, who shame other women into obedience.

Because of our work, physicians in many countries have begun to receive training to help them recognize violence as a major health risk to women. In 1985 (ten to fifteen years after feminists, including the National Women's Health Network, first sounded the alarm), the United States surgeon general issued a public health report which stated that the incidence and severity of abuse against women is epidemic, that women are not safe in their own homes. Studies suggest that violence is the major cause of injury to women aged fifteen to forty-four who are seen in an emergency room. Some physicians are being trained to diagnose and treat abused women; however, this does not mean that they, or that all physicians, actually do so. The training is neither widespread nor sufficient, the treatment available only sporadically.

Because of our work, the leaders of major religions, lawyers, judges, legislators, police departments, and insurance companies are, increasingly, recognizing male family violence and child abuse, including child sexual abuse, as a crime.

While this is a leap forward—it is also too little. The epidemic of male family violence continues, and few (male) perpetrators are ever prosecuted. United States studies suggest that only 1 percent of those arrested are actually convicted, and that few serve any time in prison. Only the few (female) victims who kill in self-defense are prosecuted, usually to the full extent of the law.

Because of our work, the international community, at least on paper, now views women's rights as *human* rights. It is understood, at least on paper, that women are entitled to freedom from violence *at home*—that this is a basic human right.

For example, in June of 1993, the Vienna Conference adopted a Declaration and Programme of Action. It called for "the elimination of violence against women in public and private life. . . . and the eradication of any conflicts which may arise between the rights of women and the harmful effects of certain traditional or customary practices, cultural prejudices, and religious extremism."

Finally, even the United Nations formally recognized violence against women as a violation of human rights. In December of 1993, the General Assembly adopted the Declaration on the Elimination of Violence against Women. The declaration included marital rape and wife-battering as forms of violence against women. The UN warned member states against "invok[ing] any custom, tradition, or religious consideration" to justify "customary," traditional violence against women.

In 1994, for the first time, in its annual report on human rights, the U.S. State Department expanded the grounds for granting asylum to include violence against women. In 1995, the U.S. Immigration and Naturalization Service recognized domestic abuse, rape, and other forms of violence against women as grounds for political asylum.

This all came about because of ongoing radical feminist work. And this work must be continued.

I hope you do just that.

However, these declarations are only pieces of paper. If a flood tide of abused women from all over the world managed, miraculously, to escape from captivity—managed, miraculously, to "find" money for travel and legal costs, without which they could not demand asylum in another country—what do you think would happen? Can the United States afford to grant asylum to one hundred thirty million women in flight from genital mutilation, who speak no English, and have no legally marketable skills? If Sweden and Belgium grant political asylum to the women battered in each country, if Egypt and South Africa or Bosnia and Rwanda exchange their rape victims—how (and who) would guarantee that the refugee women would not be similarly abused in their new (patriarchal) countries?

Creating a feminist continent might make more sense.

LETTER TWELVE

"Love Is Not Love Which Alters When It Alteration Finds."

IS YOUR LOVE FOR ANOTHER PERSON more important than your love for God or country or family? If love is about union with someone or something larger than ourselves then know the following:

No true union can succeed with half-people. Union—and transcendence—requires two whole people. This idea may be totally foreign to you since you live in a culture (patriarchy) that eroticizes social and biological differences, or opposites. This makes your task an exciting and pioneering one: to forge relationships of equality and to come to your beloved(s) whole.

So much of what passes for love is merely economic dependence. Women tend to romanticize economic and legal dependence. Perhaps men romanticize domestic and sexual-reproductive service.

Love is not love if it forces you to compromise who you are. Love is a process and a discipline. It is not only what you feel for someone else. Like freedom, it is a path, a practice, which no legal contract can guarantee or enforce.

People may live together and not love each other at all, they may abuse each other, stifle all joy. For example, many parents who say they love their children do not behave as if this were true. Some people remain together because they are terrified of loneliness, or for the sake of the children. These are not crimes, but do not confuse such human arrangements with free love.

Loving freely means first "seeing" yourself and then your beloved for who she or he uniquely is, not who you need them to be. You cannot love someone and expect them to compromise some core part of their identity because you need them by your side at every major event in your life. Loving involves letting go—and going on, sometimes alone, to those places to which your soul is drawn.

Sex and Humanity

SEXUAL PLEASURE IS NOT A SIN. Nor is it a sacrament. It is your right as a human being to exercise as you see fit. It's amazing that I feel the need to say this, but, given our times, I do.

Feminists are not—and never have been—against sexual pleasure. Patriarchy is—and has always been—against sexual pleasure *for women*. Confusing one's own sexual orgasms with radical actions is silly, pretentious. Feeling good physically is important, but it is not political in the same way as freeing prisoners from concentration camps or feeding the poor. Romanticizing female lust as Goddess-given is as dangerous as romanticizing male war lust as God-given.

If you're a woman, sex is not something you have to submit to (or aspire to) only with a man, or only with your husband, in marriage. Sexual pleasure is not necessarily tied to reproduction. If you're a man, sex is not something you can buy or take by force.

Sex is not something that you can only share with members of the opposite sex. Nor is it something that always results in genital orgasm.

As human beings, we are more than the sum of our sexual parts. However, women are more often reduced to a collection of eroticized body parts: a pretty face, cleavage, breasts, buttocks. Many parts of a woman's body can be eroticized, i.e., can become the focus of orgasm: a foot in a high-heeled shoe, an exposed back, or hip, or thigh, or calf.

In some countries, a woman's exposed (unveiled) face, her eyes, or eyebrows when seen above a half-veil, immediately suggest a forbidden vagina, an orgasm, an orgy, a brothel.

Even in our sex-saturated society, and despite an increase in teenage pregnancies, young girls today, especially of the inner cities, are not having orgasms any more frequently than the young girls of my generation ever did. I didn't believe this either, until I interviewed counselors who are working with precisely this population.

Sex education in the schools and in the media is still being hotly contested and condemned by religious fundamentalists. There is some good information available; it is hard to find. Know that most women cannot have an orgasm without direct clitoral stimulation. Both men and women enjoy oral sex. And, in the era of AIDS and other sexually transmitted diseases, people should not have unprotected sex.

But they do, they do, young people especially.

The solution to unwanted pregnancies, epidemics of sexually transmitted diseases, rape, and incest involves educating the coming generations in radically different ways. Young men must be taught to refrain from using coercion of any sort in matters sexual; young women must be taught how to resist such coercion.

The same experience—having sex—can have different consequences as a function of gender. For example, many young girls still lose their reputations for having sex; boys rarely do. (SOS—Same Old Shit.) Again, contrary to myth, women can and do sexually contract AIDS from men far more often and easily than men do from women, including from prostitutes. Women get pregnant, men don't, and mothers, no matter how young, often bear sole, lifelong responsibility for a child—more so than most fathers ever do. Women also bear the sole, lifelong trauma of having given up a child for adoption.

Sexual desire is fluid, ever-changing, especially if it's more than a masturbation fantasy. Sex may mean one thing when you're eighteen, and an entirely different thing when you're sixty-five. No, all people do not lose their desire for orgasm or affection as they age; some do though, but they're often happy about it. However, health and leisure time free of worry are essential.

You may experience desire one way with one person, another way with another person—or differently over time with the same person.

Some men may experience more sexual desire when they're young, some women when they're older; some men may think the beginnings of sexual relationships are hot, some women that it's hotter when you've come to know and trust your partner.

Trust me, sex is more complex and simpler than you've been led to believe.

Even Dr. Freud said we are all bisexual. This doesn't mean that bisexuals swing from trees, first one way, then another. It means that we all have the potential to love, mate, and experience sexual pleasure with someone of our own sex too. No big deal.

Homophobia is the last acceptable prejudice. I have observed people of all classes, races, and political persuasions bond by mocking homosexuals and lesbians, or by boasting, loudly and non-stop, of their own heterosexuality.

Telling you that I'm either heterosexual or lesbian tells you very little about how often I have genital sex, or how I have orgasms, or what sex or love really means to me. Homosexuals are not what homophobes assume. What being a lesbian means probably has little to do with our culture's general perception of a lesbian.

Both physicists and philosophers tell us that things are not what they seem—sturdy tables, for instance, are no more than molecules in motion—and that all things change, nothing remains the same.

I know women and men who were once heterosexual, parented children together, and who later became homosexuals. They still love their children, they are still good parents. I know closet homosexuals who legally married each other as cover, had children, continue to keep up the heterosexual pretense, but still prefer liaisons with others of their own sex.

Things are not always what they seem. Know that.

"Not the Church, Not the State, Women Must Decide Their Fate."

NO WOMAN SHOULD BE FORCED to have an abortion against her will. No woman should be prevented from having an abortion against her will.

This is what choice is about.

I believe in a woman's absolute right to *choose* whether and when she will have a child. Free choice means that a woman must have access to high-quality, physician-assisted, economically affordable, legal abortion *and* have the option of keeping the child she chooses to bear without having to pay an inhuman price for doing so.

Inhuman prices include: Children having children, having to drop out of school, having a child alone, without family or community, being condemned to poverty because we have no affordable day care, etc. It is also inhuman to have to surrender a child for adoption. This is a trauma from which many birth mothers never recover.

Abortion is not murder. It is the termination of a fetus. This is my view, and the view of the Supreme Court in 1973, in *Roe v. Wade*. However, if women do not have the legal right to decide whether a pregnancy is a future baby or an unacceptable burden, then it is women who are civilly dead.

Anti-abortion crusaders are more concerned with the rights of the unborn than with the rights—including the right to life—of the living. Abortion opponents actually champion the unborn at the expense of the pregnant woman and her other living children. Anti-abortionists do not demand that the state invade a *man's* body against his will for the sake of his living child—who may, for example, die without his father's kidney, lung, or bone marrow.

For at least 10,000 years of recorded history, most women were forced into biological motherhood, and, unlike men, were severely punished and sometimes killed for having sex outside of marriage.

It was therefore obvious to my generation of feminists that women needed to secure the right to safe, legal, and affordable birth control and abortions. Without them, how could a woman pursue life or liberty? She could not—and cannot. I feel as strongly about the importance of birth control and abortion today as I did thirty years ago.

Ideally, a woman's right to choose an abortion should be a civil, not just a privacy right. A woman must have the right to decide if and when to become a mother—not merely the right to choose abortion when her life or health are at stake.

Abortions have always existed. They have not always been illegal, but when they were, wealthy women had them anyway.

Poor women either didn't, or risked death at the hands of back-alley practitioners.

In the 1950s, white teenagers who couldn't find or afford an illegal abortion, or who couldn't go through with one, had to endure endless recriminations from their parents; they *had* to drop out of high school or college—no one pregnant was allowed to attend. The "lucky" teenager got to marry someone who didn't really want to marry her and who wasn't ready to be a husband and father. Or she was forced to surrender her child for adoption.

The teenage father was rarely blamed—only the mother was.

I remember thinking, ah, if you're female, one slip and you're down for the count forever. One night of experimental lovemaking, one brief affair, one tragic episode of rape—and a young woman and her child could be condemned, permanently, to lesser, harsher lives.

In 1959, I traveled alone, between college exams, for an appointment with the famed underground physician Dr. Robert Spencer, of Pennsylvania. (Rumor had it that his daughter had died of a botched, illegal abortion and that this was his way of making sure it didn't happen again to anyone else's daughter.) When I arrived, Dr. Spencer was "out of town." He frequently was. The man lived one step ahead of the law. I remember sitting on a swing in a nearby park, disconsolate, thinking that my life *as I wanted to live it* might be over if I couldn't find another abortionist.

Of course, I went to see Dr. Spencer alone, not with my boyfriend. Back then, men were not supposed to see women in curlers or cold cream, much less in childbirth or having an abortion.

Not all abortionists were trained physicians. They didn't always use anesthesia, and the pain was terrible, but you were more afraid of dying, or of having your parents find out. Some of us also had to contend with the sexual innuendos and gropings of the abortionist. The secrecy and the humiliation were profound.

Over a fourteen-year period, I had other abortions. And yes, I used birth control: first an IUD—until it became embedded in the wall of my uterus, then a diaphragm. Guess what? They failed.

Americans obtained the right to legal abortion in this country not because feminists fought and died for it, but because a sexually positive climate had been created in which both lawyers and physicians emerged who supported a woman's right to choose abortion. They had seen too many women die awful deaths from unsafe, illegal abortions. Perhaps, physicians also viewed abortion as a potentially lucrative practice. Perhaps, both men and women wanted *women* to experience sex without worry, not merely as a way to procreate.

My generation initially focused more on a woman's right to abortion than on her right to motherhood—or on the rights of racially persecuted women to resist sterilization, or the "ideal" of a small family. We were not wrong, nor were we right; no movement can do everything at once. Women were so universally obligated to become mothers, so universally condemned for pursuing independence that our feminist path was clear.

I have never softened about a woman's right to choose: not while I was pregnant, not after I gave birth to my son. I did not think that *my* right to choose to have a baby meant that *all* women had to make this same choice, nor did I think that if they didn't they were, somehow, not respecting my love for my own baby. I experience no contradiction between my *choosing* to have a child and the next woman's *choosing* not to have a child.

Make no mistake, I experienced giving birth as a sacred rite of passage.

In the late 1960s, before abortion was legal, I initiated some meetings to discuss how we could *physically* defend our then-underground clinics and networks. I should have kept notes. But who could have imagined that, only thirty years later, the right to a legal abortion would be under such deadly attack?

Never could I have imagined that, in 1997, abortion clinics and their employees would have to suffer prolonged off-site personal harassment, aggressive anti-abortion demonstrations and endless bomb threats, or that they'd be forced to install metal detectors and help train feminists to escort frightened women into and out of clinics.

Who could have foreseen that so many clinics across the country would be forced to close, would be bombed—not once, but repeatedly—that physicians and clinic workers would be forced to wear bulletproof vests, harassed, even killed so that women could exercise their rights to have a legal abortion. We could never have imagined that physicians and medical students might decide not to perform any abortions, because they seemed too dangerous, too much trouble.

Yes, freedom for women means trouble. But without such freedom, women would be in even more trouble.

Abortion has been under serious siege for more than twenty years, ever since Henry Hyde pushed through his infamous amendment to a federal funding bill that made it much harder for poor women to have federally subsidized abortions.

What can you do? There is more than one feminist thing to do. For example, a feminist might, honorably, do any of the following:

1. vote for pro-choice politicians, write them checks, and actively campaign for them;
2. escort women into and out of abortion clinics;
3. open abortion clinics—currently, at least 84 percent of U.S. counties do not have any abortion providers;
4. educate young men about their responsibilities as fathers; educate young women about their responsibilities, too;
5. pioneer research on more effective, less harmful methods of female birth control;
6. develop and distribute a male birth control pill;
7. lobby your church or religious congregation to change its stance on birth control and abortion;
8. campaign for a guaranteed above-minimum wage for all workers, so the choices are more affordable for everyone;
9. *personally* shelter, or become family to, a particular pregnant woman who wants to keep her baby, but who has no education, no money, and no family support—this option is reserved for saints;
10. become a physician willing to perform abortions; or a lawyer willing to represent physicians who perform abortions, clinic owners, and staff.

The list is endless. However, in my view, there are at least two feminist bottom lines. Rendering abortion illegal is not a feminist option, nor is forcing birth mothers to surrender their infants to adoption. Studies have persuaded me that birth mothers end up surrendering their peace of mind and mental health when they surrender their newborns for adoption. And even loved, well-cared-for adopted children suffer, psychologically, more than other children do.

Do I think the Second Wave of feminism worked as hard on obtaining the right to mother or parent under *feminist* working conditions as they did on keeping abortion legal? No, I don't. But obtaining the right to an abortion is far easier than redefining the family.

As Americans, we shun collective social solutions to what we still view as individual, private matters. We do so at our own peril.

You've inherited the consequence of our failure to redefine the family. The task is yours.

The Joys of Motherhood

DESPITE ALL MY BOOK LEARNING, when it came to motherhood, I was as naive as the next woman. I assumed that motherhood was respected and rewarded in our society. I was wrong. Motherhood was more often punished—by employers especially—or not supported by relatives and friends. ("Don't expect me to baby-sit for you. I brought my kids up totally on my own. Now you're facing the same thing. Deal with it.")

I thought my son's father could never abandon him; I was wrong. Paternal abandonment was something that my *grandmother's* generation might have feared, or expected. I didn't believe this was possible. Not *my* man, not my *feminist* man.

I thought that I, the Amazon career warrior, could abandon an infant far more easily than a feminist temporary househusband could; I was wrong, all wrong. I absolutely could not desert my infant son. I also thought I could support a child financially on my own; I was wrong, that's way too hard for any one person to do. I thought that relatives, friends, society would share or subsidize my heroic enterprise; I was wrong, that's too hard for most people to undertake.

I thought my situation was unique, and I blamed myself for making poor choices; wrong again, my situation was all too common and in no way my fault.

Learning all these things radicalized me. After all, I had given birth to a human being. After that, how seriously could I take uniforms, rank insignia?

I learned that, despite an awful lot of commercial sentimentality, motherhood itself is so powerful, so magical, that it is feared, punished, isolated, ghettoized. The experience of pregnancy and motherhood puts you in touch with a more organic, psychic way of being in the world—a way that is more despised than rewarded by our culture. I also learned that mothers did not (were not allowed to) think they were doing anything *that* special, or extraordinary.

In 1977, when I chose to become a biological mother, not one of my closest feminist comrades was pregnant or the mother of young children. Those who were mothers had grown children. Some regretted having been forced into motherhood at so early an age. Some were simply not interested in babies or children.

One night at dinner, I shared the news of my pregnancy with a feminist friend and leader. "Don't do it," she yelled. "But it's my body," I said. "Don't desert our little revolution," she implored. "It won't be that easy to get rid of me," I assured her. "You'll be sorry, this will wreck you," she warned. "My gamble," said I. (My friend was right: I was embarking on a dangerous mission.) Her lover, a mother herself, rolled her eyes and congratulated me—but only when our friend left the table.

Days later, my friend delivered an utterly charming, huge drawing as a gift apology, which she'd titled: *Phyllis during the Great Pregnancy.* Then, she and a photographer tried to persuade me to pose naked and pregnant for *Vogue* magazine. I refused. (I'm not sure if *Vogue* was really interested.) They were both commercial clairvoyants, years ahead of the naked and pregnant Demi Moore on the cover of *Vanity Fair.*

On the West Coast, some friends suggested that I give birth on top of a mountain surrounded by chanting feminist witches. They saw my pregnancy as a sacred event.

I did too.

When I became a mother, I had to *fight* for the right to have a midwife in attendance in the hospital. Maternity leave had to be *fought* for and was discouraged; paternity leave (and a father's rooming-in at the hospital) was mightily mocked. The idea of corporate flextime for two-career families had not yet been suggested. Breast-feeding was still discouraged—you couldn't do it in public without being made to feel very uncomfortable; there were no baby changing stations in public restrooms.

And this was only twenty years ago.

Many Second Wave feminists *did* understand that pregnancy, childbirth, and motherhood were great rites of passage. They became midwives, mothers, theologians, ritualists. A baby boom among both lesbians and heterosexual single women also occurred. However, it took years to get even a *minimum* level of child support legislated into existence. We found that it was still almost impossible to make (unwilling) fathers pay or relate to their children. We failed to persuade state and federal legislatures that women and children were the future of our country and, therefore, that the working conditions of parents must be improved. Workers cannot be starved, rendered homeless, denied health care and decent education.

My generation of feminists was unable to ensure every woman's right to legal, safe, affordable, and humane motherhood.

This is your struggle to continue.

Do not feel compelled to reproduce. There are many ways to have children in your life. While we do not have to become biological parents, in my view we *do* have to assume responsibility for the next generations.

Do not abandon the children you choose to have.

You do not need a child or a spouse in order to be a member of a family. You do not need the state to legally certify that you *are* a family member. You do not need to give birth to a child in order to take responsibility for a child.

However, I also believe that children need truly evolved people—not other, larger children—as parents.

Therefore, don't have a child until you've forged your own identity, can support yourself, and have already begun the work of creating or maintaining an extended family.

"Making Family" in the Modern Age

FEMINISTS HAVE REPEATEDLY BEEN DENOUNCED as being anti-family. This is not true. Feminists oppose the patriarchal family that is male-dominated, father-absent, and mother-blaming. There are some good patriarchal families: you're lucky if you come from one. Unfortunately, there are as many families in which children are physically and psychologically disfigured in such a way that they are likely to re-visit such abuse on their own children. Mothers and fathers have, traditionally, enforced gender stereotyping and gender apartheid.

The feminist ideal—and it is just that, an ideal—is a more egalitarian one. Feminists envision a variety of ideal families, not just one. People sometimes create families with friends; such families are usually not legally recognized, although they may be legally penalized. A family with children may consist of a man and a woman, both, one, or none of whom may be biologically related to the children. A family with children may also consist of same-sex adult pairs, men and women, both, one, or none of whom may be the stay-at-home primary caregiver.

I know two adult lesbians who have chosen to be surrogate grandmothers to the son and daughter of a lesbian couple. They take their responsibilities seriously, baby-sit regularly, celebrate holidays together. As far as I know, there are no screaming scenes, no drunkenness, no sudden unilateral withdrawals.

The way the experience of "family" ought to be, but often isn't.

I know some grandparents who function as their grand-children's parents—but who are also the elders of an extended family consisting of adoptive, foster, and biological children.

I know a heterosexual woman who, for years, has cultivated the children of her friends. She is blessed with many children.

What such families often have in common is less sex-role stereotyping, less authoritarianism, and more sharing of both household and economic tasks.

I believe that every citizen—no, every human being—should be entitled to health and pension coverage whether they are legally married or parents or not. We should not have to "pair up" with one other person to be entitled to certain benefits.

Despite the way feminists have been portrayed in the media, feminists understand that women, like men, long for human connectedness and stability—but rarely have it. Traditional men rarely undertake the work of making relationships or family-work. Housekeeping, child care, holiday making, and keeping in touch are what women do for others, not what others in the family do for women—not even for those women who also earn outside money.

Feminists are interested in creating families that do not overburden any one member, economically or domestically. While one's ability to sacrifice certain things for the sake of others is what civilization should be about, a feminist family model is not one based upon the unilateral sacrifice of women only.

The feminists of my generation were the ones who discovered how lonely and isolated many married mothers of young children—and grown children—really were. We discovered that wives (husbands too) are often both sexually and emotionally deprived within marriage—especially when they have young children. Fathers usually had an easier time of getting their egos and sexual needs met elsewhere. Mothers—rarely.

In my view, children need more than one or two parents; adults need more than a mate, however wonderful that mate may be. We all need an extended family—a network of people who will extend themselves to each other. Often, and for a variety of reasons, extended family no longer works in its biological form, i.e., aunts, uncles, grandparents. If we want one—we must often create it for ourselves.

It is hard to create and maintain utopian families. It might have helped if we had a variety of feminist "churches," i.e., total spiritual-political institutions to shelter us.

I want you to think about it, though. While I firmly believe that each human being needs his or her own living quarters, I must ask, can we dare to live together, share some basic costs, eliminate some of the isolation that comes with doing feminist work in the world?

But, if you think getting along with *one* spouse or set of biological parents is hard, try an embattled collective of psychologically rebellious daughter-sisters. In my generation, when we were young revolutionaries, living together often meant living in semi-squalor. No one cleaned. No one cooked. (I never did.)

Sometime in the mid-1970s, I spent the night at a feminist collective in a small rural area. I was an invited guest. And women know all about how to make a guest feel welcome, right? I could not find one clean, dry towel nor could I find more than a smidgen of peanut butter to munch on. Because this collective was health-conscious, I couldn't find coffee either. No one introduced me to anyone; anonymous female shadows kept on slithering by. These women were young, poor, sleep-deprived, shy, and suffering from too much butch attitude. They were also science fiction characters come to life: Amazons. Some practiced martial arts, some read the Tarot, all published a community newsletter, womanned a rape-crisis phone. They didn't party, they demonstrated. They were very serious about making a revolution.

I was not all that different, except I still thought it worthwhile to entertain guests properly.

I remember another feminist collective whose members all wrote sublime poetry and whose goal was to open a bookstore-cafe. Their ashtrays were always overflowing, their window shades were perpetually drawn, a writer or two could always be found drinking black coffee in a terry-cloth robe at noon. Atmospherically, it was always the other side of midnight there.

As a rule, no one mothers heroic women. Certainly not other heroic women.

Try to see if you're better at this than we were.

Few feminist collectives welcomed infants or children: boys, especially. Nor did they welcome senior citizens. It's impossible to build a family or a community if you're not intergenerational.

Remember that.

In my time, some rural feminist collectives did some glorious things together: built houses, built goddess altars, learned how to shoot, drove tractors, planted crops, fixed cars. I knew a lesbian with a Ph.D. from Harvard who for years had disappeared beneath the hood of whatever VW wasn't working—part male identification, part guilt over being middle class.

I love these women still. I will never forget them.

And then our youth ran out, the era ended, feminists moved on.

Things do not have to last forever to be good, and when they end, it is not always proof that one's principles were wrong.

Marriage: A Not-So-Sacred Institution

BRIDAL PHOTOGRAPHS and wedding stories are back in vogue. Wealthy, celebrity brides gaze adoringly at their grooms; they wear enormously expensive gowns that are, paradoxically, both sexy and virginal. The stories of how the wedding couple met and where they bought their china are presented in sophisticated and romantic vignettes. I admit it. I read these stories. Why not? The alternatives are stories of war and other human atrocities, and I still momentarily gladden at the sight of a bride who, at least for a day and despite her gender, is being treated as someone special.

Lesbians and homosexuals are also choosing marriage-like ceremonies and fighting for state-sanctioned domestic partnerships.

Marriage as we know it is not likely to disappear anytime soon. But it is certainly not a feminist institution. I do not oppose your right to choose to marry. I do oppose your going into it blindly.

By now, you've no doubt gotten the societal message: If you don't marry, you'll be doomed to a life of loneliness. No one will love you. People will think you're unnatural; selfish too. You will deny your parents and your tribe their earned, genetic immortality, and yourself the joys of children. You will have no one to grow old with, no one who'll remember you when you were young. *God* wants you to marry. Oh, and try to marry a rich man or woman, you can learn to love them just as well.

Let my voice be heard above this barrage of propaganda.

At the very least, I would like you to think about marriage before you enter into it. I never did.

No one tells you that marriage *as we know it* may actually stand in the way of what we most want from it: love, passion, respect, security, stability, continuity, growth. No one ever told me that, far from being the solution, patriarchal marriage is exceptionally dangerous for women and their children. Sometimes, a private home is the most dangerous place for a woman to be.

If, as feminist women and men, you want to create unions that are stable, felicitous, and egalitarian, you may have to forget nearly everything that you've been so carefully taught. You literally can't afford to marry or have marriage-like relationships with anyone. I am not saying you cannot love or live with each other; I am saying that you must do so for different reasons and on different terms than anything you've imagined.

Women, especially, can't afford to look for a protector or father-figure: it will do you in. We are all interdependent, but you should only make alliances with peers, not with those who are more powerful than you.

Emma Goldman said she was against marriage too—if for no other reason than it placed crowns of thorns upon the heads of innocent babes and called them bastards if their mothers weren't married.

Also, for every marriage that is made in Heaven, there is a marriage made in Hell. As you know, many marriages do not last, and many that do exact too great a price in exchange. From both men and women. However, divorce is not the solution either. A divorce does not solve our economic problems, or our need for a family and community.

I am not saying that heterosexual men and women can't or shouldn't love each other or live together or create families. Some married folk say they are very happy or happy enough with what they've got, and I have no reason to disbelieve them; some single folks say the same thing. Hear Ye: I am not saying that unmarried people are happier than married people or that impoverished single mothers are better off than a wealthy, two-parent family.

I am saying that, historically, from a feminist point of view, for thousands of years, marriage, as we know it, has been a forced, economic arrangement. On both sides. Legal marriage has often (but not always) isolated women from their families of origin and from bonding with other women, exploited women as indentured (unsalaried) live-in domestic and reproductive servants, and formerly entitled a husband to his wife's wages when she worked outside the home—and to her inheritance too.

Marriage also oppressed women sexually: until recently, a wife could not charge her husband with rape. By definition, she was his sexual and reproductive property. (If a wife alleges marital rape, she must still convince a judge and jury—no easy task.) Marriage also endangered women physically: until very recently, women couldn't allege marital battery. Women are still a long way from ending marital abuse and from winning the right to defend themselves. A traditional wife was not entitled to time off, or to lovers of her own—although she was expected to forgive her husband for straying.

Not a pretty picture.

If we only have "bad" alternatives, choosing the lesser of two evils may be the best you can do. This does not mean it is a feminist solution. A feminist solution would require finding others who are in your situation, who see things as you do, and who also want to create a feminist marriage or community.

Visible, mainstream, feminist alternatives have yet to be created.

My parents married for life. They did not expect to be happy. Their expectations were fully met. They expected to survive, economically, and to raise children. In this, they were entirely successful.

I never wanted a marriage like that, and I've never had one.

I did, however, marry: not once, but twice. The passion did not last, promises were not kept, my life was endangered. Although no harm was intended, harm was done—on both sides.

I deeply regret this.

Female Fugue States

WOMEN OFTEN ACCEPT DEFEAT as a given; they tend to pride themselves on making the best of it. Often, when a "good" woman wins "a little something"—at home or at work—she over-inflates its importance and is overly grateful for the slightest accommodation.

As a feminist, do not confuse defeat or co-optation with victory—something oppressed people often tend to do.

Do not settle for a little flattery, or token advancements.

In my generation, if our opponents paid attention to us, interviewed us, published our views, rewarded us in minimal ways, we often thought that things had improved for all women; after all, they'd improved for us, individually, hadn't they? To this day, the fate of most women remains unjust—no matter how many brilliant speeches my generation made.

Women—feminists too—enter fugue states as a way of bearing that which we do not think we can change. Verbal taunts on the street. Incest at home. We pretend it's not happening; I'm not here, it doesn't matter. This helps us survive, but it prevents us from living in our bodies, or breaking with patriarchy.

A few years ago, I attended a Bar Mitzvah party. The Bar Mitzvah boy's parents were divorced. I'd found a clutch of other uncoupled women and there we stood, all vivid and verbally riotous, arms a-bangled, fingers bejeweled, loud and laughing. I was full of myself and holding forth on many subjects (we all were), when the Bar Mitzvah boy's father, whom I'd never met, came over.

Bearded, with kind eyes, he was well-spoken, well-dressed. Here was a man, divorced, available, and on the loose in Manhattan. The single and man-hungry among us began, slightly, imperceptibly, to shift our center of gravity away from our festive female group, and towards him. The man singled me out and said, "Ooh, what you're saying excites me. Can I fuck you?"

Yes. He actually said that.

It took me a few seconds to come to my senses. But first, the long-dormant girl in me felt flattered. I'd won the beauty contest, the Prince wanted me. But what he wanted, even before he knew me, was to fuck me: as if any woman can be reduced to her sexual parts and "had." As if each of us were merely killing time, just waiting for him to choose one of us. That each of us was actually eager to leave the other laughing girls behind to clinch the deal.

We used to do this—when we were teenagers. We broke dates with each other if a boy wanted us. Broke dates? We stopped in mid-sentence, deserted each other forever, for the dubious privilege of having a boy take advantage of us. I say "take advantage" not because I'm anti-sex, but because in my day any girl who was as sexually adventurous as a boy was branded and shamed. As I was.

So it took me a full two seconds before I came to my senses. Of course, I didn't hit him. I couldn't ruin the Bar Mitzvah. I handled it like a "lady": I pretended not to hear what he'd said. We all pretended. We pretended so well that I actually had to ask one of the other women if I'd *imagined* the entire episode. We were all "ladies," long used to pretending that we could take it, whatever *it* was, without making a fuss, without telling, without even remembering, and definitely without suing, hitting, or shooting any man who'd "only" insulted or hurt us.

We automatically covered up this man's small, outrageous act. We knew better than to hold him responsible for what he said, or to shame him publicly. We were "ladies" and we wouldn't descend to his level. Also, maybe he didn't know what he was saying, maybe he meant well, maybe what he said wasn't so bad, it could have been worse, we didn't want to spoil the party. You know the litany of justification.

Women "forget" what frightens us. We do not mobilize against it. Feminists too are susceptible to such erasures.

It's 1993, and I'm meeting with some other veteran feminists. I love these women, we go way back, they're like relatives whom I never had enough time for, and now I want to know them better: the price they paid, and how they're doing now. I'm moved by how much softer, sadder, smaller, we all are, but fragrant with history, sacred—like the little goddess figurines in a glass museum case in Crete. Incredibly, we're all still defiant. And longing for each other, and for action.

So, we're talking about what we have—feminist conscious-ness—and what we don't have—action, money, health, commu-nity—and about how we thought that by now we'd have a revolution, and how defeated we feel by each daily detail that traps us. We feel grounded, as if we're adolescents trapped in aging bodies, or angels: winged, immortal, who can no longer fly, but who've lost the knack for ordinary life.

And then it's Marion's turn to speak. She says, "I killed a man, he was my father, and he'd been raping me all my life, and so, finally, one day, when I was sixteen, I resisted, we struggled, I hit him hard, and he fell backwards, down the stairs, and by the time he hit bottom, he was dead."

Utter silence. No one fidgeted, got up for more coffee, cleared her throat, smoothed her hair, reached for a tissue, or whispered anything to her neighbor.

"My mother treated the incident as an accident, which, in a sense, it was, but I was glad he was dead. The police never pressed charges."

And then, for a blessed hour, we stopped thinking of ourselves, and became animated, focused, we were laughing and talking, our cheeks got rosier, and energy filled our every limb. Did this mean that as a group, we would back incest victims who killed their fathers in self-defense? Were we at long last ready to expand the definition of self-defense for women?

Two or three weeks passed before we met again. I asked several group members what they thought of Marion's story. One woman said, "Are you referring to something in particular? After all, we all said a lot of things." A second woman responded, "Didn't she throw a man down the stairs, a burglar, I think that's who it was." A third woman, "I don't remember what she said. Didn't she have a problem with the police, or was it with her mother, is that it?"

No joking. Mass amnesia. Animation all gone, affect dissociated.

"Have you all gone mad?" I asked. And I reminded them of precisely what Marion had said. "Oh, yes, you're quite right, how silly to forget it. Well, we didn't really forget it. But we have other things to talk about tonight."

As women, we're supposed to absorb injury and humiliation every day. Few women ever say "here is where I draw the line." When we do, it puts other women on notice about their own lives, it makes them uncomfortable. Why are women so proud of our ability to take it? Female machisma.

What have they done to us? What have we done to ourselves?

A woman is brave when she knows what can be done to her but, in spite of such knowledge, manages to help other women anyway. A woman is brave when she is able to do combat with the "good little girl" within, the voice that says mind your own business, tend to your own garden, don't help, you'll get in trouble, you'll get caught, you'll be sorry, you'll be punished, *no one will like you.*

Where are our freedom fighters? Where are our heroes ready to be dropped behind enemy lines? We are still too few in number to make much of a difference. Are women so disassociated from our bodies, and from each other, that simple resistance terrorizes us more than our daily dose of humiliation and death? Are most women so opportunistic, so cowardly that we are willing to die for our Masters but not live for ourselves?

I certainly hope not.

Boundaries

"NICE" GIRLS DON'T HIT. Nice girls mind their manners. Nice girls sit with their knees close together, try to take up as little space in the universe as possible. Nice girls are not supposed to raise their voices. Nice girls marry men who are supposed to do it for them.

People are more terrified of the power of women's repressed rage than of men's military weapons. We feel that women's anger can destroy the world. We often overlook or minimize the consequences of male anger.

I was thirty-three years old before I ever hit another woman. It was the winter of 1973-74, and for months, I'd been telling all our friends that I felt as if Ellen had hit me, and unless she explained herself, I was going to hit her back. Physically. I was clear, I was direct—all nice girl "no-no's."

So when I unsuspectingly walked into a party—and there she was, I nearly walked out, but then it was too late. Ellen saw me, and she just looked away, sneaky-like, defensive. Perhaps if she'd come up to me to talk I'd have been too embarrassed to act on my threats, but she didn't. What I did was both dumb and daring.

So, it was POW! Right in the kisser. I didn't hit her very hard. She could have hit me back, and it would have ended right there. But she didn't—so I hit her again. POW! Right in the kisser. Her boyfriend just looked on, tapped his pipe, and asked, "Who is this woman, darling?"

Oh, what a brouhaha! Emergency rooms, police reports, threatened criminal and civil court actions, etc. Feminist phones rang all over town. Women who, only yesterday, had been quoted as calling for "blood in the streets," and for the "castration of rapists" were astounded, hysterical, because I, a woman, had hit a woman—two times, no lasting damage, but in public—and for political reasons. If I'd been a man, they'd probably have said, "He's under so much pressure, we didn't see who threw the first punch, they'd both had too much to drink, no harm done, let's forget it."

If I'd been a man and stabbed my wife, or thrown her out the window, or cut her up into little pieces, people might say: We weren't there, we don't know what happened, she drove him to it, she deserved it, she emasculated him, she shopped too much, she was fucking another man, and anyway, he's a genius, he's remorseful, he's a schmuck, he's our friend, our meal ticket, our darling boy.

I was struck by how everyone focused only on my visible punches, and not at all on the invisible blow that I'd sustained. Ellen had only behaved the way nice girls behave toward each other. I was at fault because I'd lost my machisma, i.e., the ability to absorb and engage in the unacknowledged competitiveness, verbal abuse, and absence of ethics that passed for business as usual among too many women.

The funny thing is that once I'd hit Ellen, it cleared the air between us, and we literally became the best of friends. Only after I'd hit her, only after I'd hurt her too, just as she'd hurt me, could I bear to hear her tale of childhood woe, the presumed basis for her awful behavior. It's not that I understood or forgave Ellen, but rather, from that moment on, we experienced each other as intimates.

We felt as if we'd grown up together, or had once been lovers. At the time, we were both still good-girl straight women. I had a husband and she had a boyfriend, and thus, our sudden intimacy felt uncanny, magical. I'd broken a taboo: women are not supposed to *touch* each other physically, not in rage, and not in lust. I had, and we'd both lived to tell the tale. We'd learned that sometimes words aren't enough, that bad manners aren't that bad, that women expressing anger—even physically— doesn't destroy the world, that we didn't have to walk around harboring permanent grudges.

From that moment on, Ellen and I both understood Valerie Solanas's point in the SCUM Manifesto: that most white, middle-class, educated women won't do anything perceived as not nice, or that *might* get them into trouble. They'd been socialized and schooled to function only in indirect, underhanded ways, behind the scenes, policing each other, not the institutions of male power. They'd never step into history, only into line.

Your body and your mind are, together, your primary country of allegiance. As a feminist, you must know—and know how to defend—your country and its boundaries.

My generation of women was trained to make ourselves available to others; men were allowed to put themselves first without being called selfish or punished for it. As a feminist woman, you must make sure you are not altogether available, i.e., easy to invade against your will. By men. By other women. By those in crisis—including your own young children.

Can you do this?

As a feminist man, you must learn not to automatically turn to women as your sole maternal resource, but to become that resource for yourself and for others, both male and female.

We must each carry our own weight. We are, collectively, only as strong as our weakest link.

If we do not command strong non-patriarchal selves, our offers of help are only minimally useful. If we are each not strong enough to take care of ourselves, our collective endeavors cannot succeed.

It is up to each of us—and all of us—to stop the violence against women and children. I am not suggesting vigilante revenge squads. I am suggesting that feminists try to understand—really understand—that no one will rescue women and children but ourselves. And if we don't know how to do that, we'd better start thinking about it.

Should feminists learn to physically defend themselves and others, then hire themselves out to other women and children? Well, why not?

Understand that as feminists you must *also* learn how to practice compassion towards adult women, how to lead, how to follow, how to be team players in order to accomplish those goals that cannot be achieved alone. (Many male feminists may already have a strong sense of self because they are men; they may need to balance things in the opposite direction.)

In order to bond with others, we must each bring some of the *same,* not only comparable skills, to the table.

Most—not all, just most—adult men tend to be taller and wider than most adult women. Male voices are naturally deep and trained to command. Unlike women, men are taught to go for it, to beat out the next guy without an apology or a single backward glance. When a man sits down, he makes himself comfortable, spreads his legs. Women are taught to sit, legs crossed, body bent-in.

Unbelievably, women tend to make way on the sidewalk for a brisk male stroller. Women "pretend" that verbal abuse has not happened, walk quickly, eyes cast down, on all the streets of the world. Most women in high heels cannot outrun a man: in pursuit of a job, a taxi, or to escape from a rapist. A man usually has more leisure time at his disposal. He is not often preoccupied about being ugly, too fat, too thin, too hairy, the way so many women are. Ugly men are seen as having character; any woman who is less than (artificially) ideal is denigrated as a dog.

If a woman decides to take up space, do more of the talking than the listening, she'll probably be seen as a bitch or a dyke. But she won't be lonely if there are many more women like her.

Once you start taking your space, be prepared to be called all kinds of names: uppity, hostile, arrogant, egotistical, angry, uptight, and unladylike. You may be shunned, or blamed for anything bad that happens to you.

So what? Being "nice" hasn't gotten women very far. Has it?

Still, the fear of being verbally shamed, then shunned, is why so many young women have learned to say, "I'm not a feminist but . . ." This strategy doesn't work. Whether or not you call yourself a feminist, I would like you to learn to stand up for whatever or whomever our culture is shaming and shunning. Don't follow the example of generations of young women who have said "I'm not a feminist but . . ." in the hope that their own individual lives would be improved because they refused to think strategically. Whether you have personally experienced any discrimination or persecution, whether or not you allow yourself to be aware of it, sexism is real, it exists, bad things *do* happen to good people—and we are all connected.

While I want you to become independent, I also want you to become strong team players. I want you to celebrate your differences, not merely tolerate them. You must each create a self, keep it strong, develop a strong sense of boundaries, stop violating other peoples' boundaries, stop allowing anyone to violate your own. In college, I dared to post a sign on my dormitory door that read: "Time is life. Anyone who wastes my time is killing me. Please don't!"

If you need to be rescued by someone, become that someone yourself. Become Princess Charming. She is you.

Telling

SOMETIMES, families choose one member as their victim, whom they then proceed to scapegoat without mercy or reason. It's almost impossible to reverse this process once it's underway. Try and stop the persecutors, and they'll turn on you, or evade you, expertly. Such families would rather exile, or even kill, their Bad Seed than allow anyone to show her (or him) the slightest tenderness.

You tell, they cover you in shit, you smell so bad, no one ever believes you again. You tell, they throw you out of their family, and it's the only family you're ever going to have. You tell, they threaten your life. From their point of view, it's what *you've* done to them. Blown the whistle on the whole scam. You're ahead if you get out alive, but you can't get out whole. You tell, and your middle-class feminist friends all look at you as if you're crazy. "Your cousin took a Mafia contract out on your life? Are you serious? You must be exaggerating. You're joking, aren't you?"

Yeah. Have another canapé to you too.

I have a cousin who used to live next door. He was still quite young when I left the neighborhood. When he was twenty, my cousin was in a terrible car accident and in a coma for a month. Afterwards, he was never the same. He flew into red rages, became sexually promiscuous—he even propositioned me.

When my cousin was thirty, he acquired a girlfriend and passed for promising. She lost fifty pounds and passed for light. They both passed for normal, and they were married. Within months, they turned back into themselves. She gained weight, he humiliated her about it. She shopped, he brought whores home. She refused to work but expected a high standard of spending. He earned, he earned, but his contempt for her grew. He began to hate her and curse her and beat her.

She always forgave him. She never told anyone.

My cousin was always getting into arguments at work and losing his job. His wife was always putting together new resumes for him, driving him to airports where he'd catch a flight for a new job interview. I visited my cousin only three times. The first time, I turned up, unexpectedly, with a boyfriend. My cousin actually chased the man out, turned on me, his face contorted with rage, as if I were his wife and he'd caught me cheating on him. I got the hell out of there, fast.

A long time passed. I told myself, maybe I'd exaggerated what I'd experienced. I still remember my cousin as a toddler when he tried to follow me everywhere—how he cried when his mother stopped him—but this was long ago, when he still had long curls, and such a sweet trusting smile.

My cousin and his wife fought constantly. By the time I saw them next, she hated him. He hated her more. They used whatever weapons they had against each other. She had a sharp tongue. He had one too, but he also had his fists and his body. He hit, she shopped, she shopped, he whored, she ate. And ate. How frantically she ate.

I told my cousin to get out, to see a psychiatrist. I told his wife the same thing. Fat chance, they were in this thing until one of them died or they killed each other.

They moved to a new city. They bought an expensive home, joined the right clubs. She spent her days shopping and caring for the house and their daughter. She was a stay-at-home wife and mother, just what my cousin had wanted. She did gourmet cooking, loved to entertain.

She was married to the house. She refused to leave it, the house was all she had. It displayed her fine china, fluffy towels, carpets, mirrored bedroom set. She would not go—no matter how often he banged her head on the floor, banged her head against the wall, gave her a black eye, locked her in her bedroom, removed the door to the bedroom after *she* installed a lock against him, threw away her crutches after she broke her leg running away from him—no, she wasn't going to let him win or make her admit that the marriage was a mini-Auschwitz. She clung to that gas chamber wall. She would not be moved.

Until their daughter told the neighbor that her father was putting his penis on her stomach.

Then, my cousin's wife called me—lucky me—hysterical. I told her to take the child, leave the house, go directly to the airport—don't even pack, just leave the state. We'd try to handle this like a family that functioned well. Instead, she told my cousin exactly what I'd said. She thought it would win her points. With him. What she got was a divorce and custody battle from hell.

The therapist who reported my cousin for child abuse called me first, since I was an expert in such cases. "Do what you have to do," said I. But then, when my cousin began to stalk the therapist, she called me again, frightened. Again, I said, "Do what you have to do."

The therapist left the state entirely.

My cousin allegedly continued to stalk her.

My cousin's wife finally fled to a shelter for battered women. My cousin thought I had personally funded that particular shelter, his wife's defection, and his potential loss of his daughter. Then, when I refused to lie on the stand for my cousin's sake, that's when he called the Mafia. That's when his mother blamed me for destroying the family. For a long time, she refused to talk to me. Then, when she did, she spent much of our time together blaming me for having sided with the woman who had destroyed her family.

I've never seen my cousin again. His mother no longer mentions him except when she sighs and says that I've hurt him.

I love her—my cousin too, but my honor and my sanity demand that I tell, not deny, these sad family truths.

I said, you can tell, and you can get out, but not whole. I may have left my family—but I was quick to rush into the arms of many a Godfather, each of whom I hoped would turn out to be my Good Mother. Some actually were, but some weren't.

Back in the mid-1960s, before feminism, I was involved with a Prince of Darkness. To this day, I still refer to him as "Morris the Monster."

Morris was an internist, and ten years older than I. He had never before lived with a woman. We'd met at a medical school, where I was a student, and he was a professor. I thought I'd finally done something right. Morris was a Jewish doctor, the kind of man I was supposed to marry. Morris's role required very little of him: a little exquisite lovemaking, some sophisticated weekends in the country, a few visits to museums, a concert or two—and I was hooked, reeled in, ready to flop around helplessly, for years, on grim ice.

Morris was a master of sadism. The more he humiliated me, the harder it was to leave him. No one told me, "Get out, it's dangerous, he's a killer." None of Morris's many judge, lawyer, physician, or professor friends, or their wives—men and women in their late thirties and early forties— *grown-ups* with whom we socialized—ever said, "Be careful, you're young, and too trusting. We've never known Morris to make a commitment to a woman, he's never been faithful, God help you if you 'land' him, he's a real woman-hater, run for your life."

I hadn't a clue. Back then, women were entirely on their own. We didn't share such essential truths with one another. I was twenty-five years old. I gave Morris my youth. He took it away from me, everyone saw the transaction going down, no one rushed in to save me from myself or from him. So I started drinking, and doing drugs. I thought of suicide—what woman hasn't?—because although I wanted to, I couldn't give up the dream of me properly married—the very dream that was killing me.

Understand: there were good times, days of pleasure in East Hampton, on Shelter Island, in Ulster County farmhouses, and in Manhattan skyscrapers overlooking both the Hudson and the East rivers. We socialized mainly with Morris's friends, not mine, we went to plays and movies and analyzed them afterwards; we talked about his research, and about his laboratory technicians, one of whom was in love with him, and how he couldn't give her up: the work she was doing for him was too important. We talked about my poems and short stories, my graduate school classes, about the meaning of life. Two modern, attractive, educated people. In love. Living together.

But, behind closed doors, Morris had temper tantrums that lasted for hours. He gave me "silent treatments" that lasted for *weeks*. Morris conducted military searches for dust and for dryness in the air; he found suitable punishments for my willful failures to fill up the radiator pans with water. He'd wake me up at 3 A.M., to show *me* how it felt to be disturbed. He'd hide my makeup, destroy my exam notes, slap me. *I'd get a kitchen knife when he did that,* I had that much spirit, and he'd walk out, quickly, and disappear for a few days, to teach me a lesson.

This was a problem that had no name. This wasn't even seen as a problem—lots of men were like this, you just had to learn to take it, or leave, and if you stayed, you lost the right to complain. Morris's friends acted as if nothing were wrong, as if Morris had the right to do whatever he could get away with. They were the only adults I knew. If something were really wrong, I told myself, they'd say something, wouldn't they? As it turned out, *all* of Morris's married friends, except one, were also having affairs, while their wives struggled with young children and desperate jealousies of their own.

One day, almost as an aside, Morris made it clear that of course he had a mistress, someone twenty years older than I was. A good woman, who did all his typing for him and who wanted so little for herself. He wasn't about to desert her for some childish whim of mine. I'd get used to it.

I was Colette, he was Willy. I was free to write about Morris's European past, among the grand, gay literati, and about the Polaroid pictures he took of us, of me, in pornographic performance, and about the "threesomes," *his* solution to the problem of male sexual boredom. "Puss," he'd say, "Don't be so noisy, calm down. If you're patient, you'll have what you want."

I left him the day I received my Ph.D. I moved out. I left everything behind. To my surprise, Morris turned up at my new apartment in Greenwich Village. He was very angry. He said I'd taken something that belonged to him and he wanted it back: a large wooden spoon, or a bowl, one that he'd especially liked. I didn't have it. Morris seemed more lost than angry, now that I'd deserted my whipping-girl post, made my getaway.

If you find yourself in this same position, I hope you'll do the same: flee, move on, move into feminism.

Economic Independence

NO WOMAN can afford to rely on others to support her economically.

In 1928, Virginia Woolf said that a woman needs the (now-quaint) sum of 500 pounds per annum and a room of her own. I second the sentiment and up the ante. A woman needs a career of her own, too—she needs to become skilled at something she takes pride in, does well, and for which she is economically rewarded.

A woman needs to be economically independent more than she needs a lover or a child. Actually, an independent income will minimize a woman's vulnerability when she embarks on either marriage or motherhood.

Work like hell to have a career locked into place before you're thirty. You should not marry or have a child until then.

Economic dependence and real—or feigned—ignorance about money or power is not an effective means of acquiring or redistributing them. Money is the most powerful of forces, but not equally so for everyone. For example, the same amount of money purchases less and has a diminished value for an African American man or woman in America, as it did for a Jew in Nazi Germany, or does now for a woman anywhere in the world.

Individually wealthy Jews in Nazi Germany could sometimes purchase their own lives—and a limited number of other Jewish lives—provided they fled the country, leaving their property and money behind. All the Jewish money in the world could not buy a respected or safe place, in the Nazi world, for individual Jews or for Jews as a group. All the African-, Hispanic-, Asian-, or Native-American money in the world cannot buy a respected or safe place within a racist country for people of color, either as individuals or as a group. All the female money in the world cannot buy a respected or safe place for women either as individuals or as a group within a misogynist country. As of this writing, there is still no feminist embassy or mission that can grant women—or men—political asylum. Understanding this concept, or putting it to use, is a measure of how well feminists will have utimately understood the use of money and power on earth.

In my time, many feminists who mounted platforms felt compelled to promise everyone—themselves especially, that feminism would solve the problems of both every conceivable persecuted group—and of their persecutors as well.

Let me be clear: Feminism is *women's* liberation struggle. In the short run, it is supposed to help women (and our male allies) fight back in the war against women. In the long run, it may end that war—a good day, if it ever comes.

I would be playing it safe, and failing you, if I insisted that feminism is a "feel good" vision that will help everybody immediately. I won't do that.

In order to free even one woman—or man—feminists must control the means of production and reproduction somewhere on earth. We must also control the armed forces and organized religions.

Do I frighten you with such militant talk? I hope so and I hope not. It is important for feminists to understand power.

Good will alone cannot airlift the woman about to be gang-raped out of Bosnia or Rwanda. We'd need an armed and diplomatic force to do that. More than twenty years ago, I interviewed women, including feminists, about what they thought a lot of money or power was. Most thought in terms of themselves, only. No one considered what it might cost to purchase and maintain even one feminist government airplane for rescue missions, what it would cost to build housing and provide health care for, let's say, a half million people. Most of my interviewees thought that female Hollywood stars had a lot of power (for women, is what they meant).

Being *seen*—dancing for daddy—ah, how often women tend to confuse the beautiful appearance, the social triumph, the group affiliation with power. While everyone today is insane about the importance of being on TV and the benefits of being famous, women are insane in a different way: it's as if we believe that if only we're seen, our every need will be met.

I once watched a woman systematically follow a hired photographer at a conference to ensure that she'd turn up in every photo. (No, she wasn't participating in the conference in any other way.) I know a woman who crashes feminist parties, softly glides into photo opportunities, then, carefully, obsessively mounts the photos and tells tall tales back home about her intimate involvement with the "stars." She is usually believed, fawned over.

Try vanishing the Catholic church's assault on women's reproductive rights by being in pictures with celebrities. Try preventing rape. Better still, try feeding the poor with a wave or two of notoriety. My point: the kind of power that can do this is simply not within the province of token numbers of celebrities.

In my view, feminist power is not the kind of power that can be achieved for oneself alone but also for the greater good and freedom of all.

Get on with this. Don't make the same mistake some women of my generation so often made, namely, confusing television appearances or publishing contracts with real power, and then fighting amongst yourselves for that tiny bit of public attention. What matters is that you gain more and more control of the institutions that serve us all so poorly.

Heroism is our only feminist alternative.

Letter to a Young Feminist Who Happens to Be a Man Who Happens to Be My Son

MY BELOVED BOY:

Do I desert the cause of women because I address you in so passionate a voice? I think not, but in my time, many feminists would have thought so. Forgive them. Understand: We were trying to practice *preferring* women. You can't imagine how much mothers, not just fathers, preferred sons to daughters and how deadly this slight was, how it injured us, reverberated through the years of our lives. I was lucky. Many others were not. In some countries, girls are killed at birth, receive less food, no education, and are sold into slavery at an early age.

In my day, few anti-feminist women really liked men. They feared, despised, respected, and obeyed male intimates and experts, but experienced men as Others. As individuals, some women sought to take advantage of La Difference through sexual wiles or by emitting learned passivity and dutifulness.

Avoid such women. They are ancient, but not honorable, history. They are still very much with us.

In my time, many feminist women did not like men either—including men who said they were feminists. Some feminist women sought a new identity—perhaps safety from violence at male hands—in separatism. Some separatists had the fond and feckless hope that it would be easier to shine among women-only. (It wasn't.) And that there would be enough love among women-only to go round forever. (There wasn't.)

Some feminist men of my generation were more weird than wondrous. Some exaggerated women's strength and thought it would protect them. Some feminist men had nothing but contempt for women and sought to dominate and destroy them. As I've said before: it is hard, even for feminists, to practice what we preach.

Do not be surprised if some feminist women reject you simply because you're a man—or worse, follow you blindly for the same reason.

I am impressed that you prize poetry and friendship and have friends who are both male and female. When I was your age, that was impossible.

I am thrilled that you've turned out to be a passionate feminist. But your education as a warrior/healer has only just begun.

For example, as I have already cautioned you: Don't shame others, women especially, whose feminism may be new, more tentative, than your own. Speak softly to them. Remember that many women are used to letting a man do the talking, used to following his lead, not used to working with men as equals, but only as their subordinates, rarely as their superiors.

Start recruiting men. Never stop.

But you have other tasks too. For example, you must learn to speak up when your men friends refer to (or treat) women as cunts or bitches—or when your women friends gossip or move against a woman in ways that are unforgivable. This is very hard to do and will break your heart: not just once, but many times. You will jeopardize a great deal if, behind closed doors, among intimates, you *privately* speak up for a particular woman. Or stand up for her, take her side, dare to support her, go after her abuser—even if he's her father, or your boss.

Your feminist consciousness (of which you're so proud) will also cause you pain. How could it be otherwise? For example, it might make you aware of unpardonable, curdling flaws among your most cherished friends. You may continue to love them, but you may also withdraw from them. And they from you.

You may have to proceed on your own, without any of the patriarchal privileges vouchsafed to men. This does not worry me too much. I would really be wringing my hands if you were a bully or a completely shallow fellow.

You are quite forceful, but you're also a very gentle soul. Therefore, you may be treated as if you're a "fag"—even if you're not, perhaps, especially if you're not.

Ah, but you must be true to who you are, no matter whom you choose to sleep with or love. I am thinking of your magical, twinkling forebearers: light-bringers, alchemists, wizards, shamans, mystics, psychics, the whole line of non-macho wise men and healers.

As Amazon knights, you may not have to psychologically desert your mothers. You may carry us with you into battle; we are already part of how you experience yourselves. If you take the heroes' road, you may do so in a new way. You must write your own scripts; there can be more than one. Perhaps one involves coming home as opposed to leaving home.

I wish you brave companions on that road. A pleasant time on earth, not one consumed in fire and eaten away by plagues; a green and summery time.

I think things will be much harder than this—but they may be easier too.

Go gently into the day. Honor your idealism, resist cynicism. Keep your heart open to the world, try and make the world better. Don't give up.

And don't forget to send me postcards from the future.

Bibliography

My generation knew nothing of the rich and radical feminist literature that preceded *Women and Madness* by more than a century. Much of the radical feminist literature of my Second Wave generation was "lost" by the 1980s. I have included some of it here. As you read this, please remember that many of the classic feminist works with which you may be most familiar were often   preceded by the most amazing and exciting speeches, pamphlets, journals, articles, and books, many of which have since been forgotten.

I have divided this bibliography into pre-twentieth century texts, pre-1962 texts, and then into seven-year periods, beginning in 1963, when Gloria Steinem and Betty Friedan both published works that would have a lasting influence. I have also included some—but not all—of the early feminist literature, including *Notes from the First Year* and *No More Fun and Games: A Journal of Female Liberation,* which were published in 1968. By the early 1970s, in every major U. S. city, feminists began publishing newspapers and journals: *Aphra, Amazon Quarterly, Big Mama Rag, Bread and Roses, Lesbian Ethics, Sojourner, 13th Moon, Quest,* and *Women: A Journal of Liberation.*

Since the late 1960s, some feminist writers have written anywhere from five to fifteen books each; few have remained continuously in print. These writers are usually remembered, if at all, for one book only: either their first or their most recent book. Even in this bibliography, I have not taken the liberty of printing each writer's entire oeuvre. I have not even included every single worthy author. That task remains. However, let me note that the following feminist writers have all written important Second Wave books—or have written many more books and articles than I've cited here:

Alta, Louise Armstrong, Margaret Atwood, Kathy Barry, Pauline Bart, Louise Bernikow, Charlotte Bunch, Paula Caplan, Suzy McKee Charnes, Kim Chernin, Nancy Chodorow, Blanche Weisen Cook, Claire Coss, Nancy Cott, Mary Daly, Andrea Dworkin, Barbara Ehrenreich, Ellen Frankfurt, Marilyn French, Sally Gearheart, Paula Giddings, Sandra Gilbert, Carol Gilligan, Linda Gordon, Vivian Gornick, Lois Gould, Susan Griffen, Susan Gubar, Bertha Harris, Molly Haskell, Shere Hite, Sarah Lucia Hoagland, bell hooks, Jill Johnston, Audre Lorde, Catharine MacKinnon, Joan Mellon, Kate Millett, Robin Morgan, Joan Nestle, Julia Penelope, Marge Piercy, Letty Cottin Pogrebin, Minnie Bruce Pratt, Arlene Raven, Janice Raymond, Adrienne Rich, Barbara Katz Rothman, Joanna Russ, Diana E.H. Russell, Barbara Seaman, Elaine Showalter, Alix Kates Shulman, Barbara Smith, Dale Spender, Kate Stimpson, Alice Walker, Barbara Walker, Lenore Walker, Monique Wittig.

The works in this bibliography are alphabetized according to author. Please note that certain lesser known books often precede a later, more visible work by anywhere from one to five years.

Pre-Twentieth Century

Behn, Alphra. *Love Letters between a Nobleman and His Sister.* Edited by Janet Toad. London, New York: Penguin Books, 1996. Originally published between 1684-1687.

———. *Oroonoko: An Authoritative Text, Historical Backgrounds, Criticism.* Edited by Joanna Lipkiny. New York: W.W. Norton, 1973. Originally published as *Oroonoko, or the Royal Slave* in 1688.

———. *The Works.* Edited by Montague Summers. New York: Phaeton Press, 1967.

Catherine II, Empress of Russia. *The Memoirs of Catherine the Great.* Edited by Dominique Maroger. Translated by Moura Budberg. New York: Collier Books, 1961. Originally published in 1781.

de Pisan, Christine. *The Book of the City of Ladies.* Translated by Earl Jeffrey Richards. New York: Persea Books, 1982. Originally published circa 1400.

Douglass, Frederick. "The Rights of Women." 28 July 1848, *North Star.*

DuBois, Ellen Carol, ed. *Elizabeth Cady Stanton, Susan B. Anthony: Correspondence, Writings, Speeches 1815-1906.* New York: Schocken Books, 1981.

Gage, Matilda Joslyn. *Woman, Church and State.* New York: The Arno Press, 1972. Orginally published in 1893.

Gilman, Charlotte Perkins. *Women and Economics.* New York: Charlton, 1898.

Herzl, Theodor. *The Jewish State: An Attempt at a Modern Solution of the Jewish Question.* New York: Dover, 1988. Originally published in 1896.

Machiavelli, Niccolò. *The Prince.* Translated by George Bull. London: Penguin Books, 1961. Originally published in 1525.

Mill, John Stuart. *The Subjection of Women.* Mineola, New York: Dover, 1997. Originally published in 1869.

Murasaki, Shikibu. *The Tale of Genji.* Translated by Arthur Waley. New York: The Modern Library, 1960. Originally published circa 998.

Paine, Thomas. "An Occasional Letter on the Female Sex."*The Complete Writings of Thomas Paine.* 2 vols. Edited by Philip S. Foner. New York: Citadel, 1945. Originally published in August 1775.

Shonagon, Sei. *The Pillow Book of Sei Shonagon.* Translated and edited by Ivan Morris. New York: Penguin Books, 1967. Originally published circa 992.

Stanton, Elizabeth Cady. *Eighty Years & More: Reminiscences 1815- 1897.* New York: Schocken Books, 1971. Originally published in 1898.

Stanton, Elizabeth Cady, and the Revising Committee. *The Women's Bible.* Seattle, Washington: Coalition Task Force on Women and Religion, 1974. Originally published in 1895.

Truth, Sojourner. "Arn't I a Woman?" Reissued as *Narrative of Sojourner Truth. A Bondswoman of Olden Time, Emancipated by the New York Legislature in the Early Part of the Present Century, with a History of Her Labors and Correspondence Drawn from Her "Book of Life."* Edited by Margaret Washington. New York: Vintage Books, 1993. Originally published in 1850.

Tzu, Sun. *The Art of War.* Translated by Samuel B. Griffith. London: Oxford University Press, 1963.   Originally published circa fourth century B.C.E.

Wollstonecraft, Mary. *The Vindication of the Rights of Woman.* Harmondsworth, Middlesex, England: Penguin Books, 1982. Originally published in 1792.

1900-1962

Beard, Mary R. *Woman as a Force in History.* New York: Collier Books, 1962.

Briffault, Robert. *The Mothers: The Matriarchal Theory of Social Origins.* Edited by Gordon Rattray Taylor. 3 vols. New York: H. Fertig, 1993. Originally published in 1931.

de Beauvoir, Simone. *The Second Sex.* New York: Vintage Books, 1989. Originally published in 1949.

Diner, Helen. *Mothers and Amazons.* Edited and translated by John Philip Lundin. New York: Julian Press, 1965.   Originally published in the 1930s under the pen name Sir Galahad.

Gilman, Charlotte Perkins. *The Living of Charlotte Perkins Gilman. An Autobiography.* New York: Arno Press, 1972.   Originally published in 1935.

Goldman, Emma. *Living My Life.* 2 vols. New York: Dover Publications, 1970. Originally published in 1931.

Herschberger, Ruth. *Adam's Rib.* New York: Pellegrini & Cudahy, 1948.

Horney, Karen. *Feminine Psychology.* New York: W. W. Norton & Co., 1967. Originally published between 1922-1937.

Levi, Primo. *Survival in Auschwitz: The Nazi Assault on Humanity.* New York: Collier Books, 1961. Originally published in 1958.

Memmi, Albert. *Portrait of a Jew.* Translated by Elisabeth Abbott. New York: Viking, 1971. Originally published in 1962.

Pankhurst, Emmeline. *My Own Story.* London: Eveleigh Nash, 1914.

Rilke, Rainer Maria. *Letters to a Young Poet.* Translated by Herter Norton. New York: W. W. Norton & Co., 1934. Originally published between 1903-1908.

Smedley, Agnes. *Daughter of Earth.* New York: The Feminist Press at the City University of New York, 1987. Originally published in 1929.

Woolf, Virginia. *A Room of One's Own.* New York: Harcourt, Brace & World, 1957. Originally published in 1929.

———. *Three Guineas.* New York: Harcourt Brace & World, 1966. Originally published in 1938.

1963-1970

Abbott, Sidney and Barbara Love. *Sappho Was a Right-On Woman: A Liberated View of Lesbianism.* Stein and Day, 1970.

Amatniek, Kathy. "Funeral Oration for the Burial of Traditional Womanhood." *Notes from the First Year.* New York: New York Radical Women, June 1968. See in addition: Shulamith Firestone, "The Women's Rights Movement in the U. S."; Anne Koedt, "The Myth of the Vaginal Orgasm."

Bart, Pauline B. "Portnoy's Mother's Complaint." *Trans-action.* November-December 1970.

Chesler, Phyllis. "Women and Psychotherapy." *The Radical Therapist.* September 1970.

Daly, Mary. *The Church and the Second Sex.* Boston: Beacon Press, 1968. Reissued with a "Feminist Post-Christian Introduction" in 1975 and with "New Archaic Afterword" in 1985.

Densmore, Dana. *Chivalry—the Iron Hand in the Velvet Glove*. Pittsburgh: Know, Inc. Pamphlet, 1969.

———. "On Celibacy." *No More Fun and Games: A Journal of Female Liberation*. Somerville, Massachusetts: October 1968. See in addition: Roxanne Dunbar, "Slavery" and "Dirge for White America."

Ellman, Mary. *Thinking about Women*. New York: Harcourt, Brace and World, 1968.

Fanon, Frantz. *Black Skin, White Masks*. New York: Grove Press, 1967.

———. *A Dying Colonialism*. Translated by Haakon Chevalier. New York: Grove Press, 1965.

Firestone, Shulamith. *The Dialectics of Sex*. New York: William Morrow, 1970.

Firestone, Shulamith, ed. and Anne Koedt, assoc. ed. *Notes from the Second Year: Major Writers of the Radical Feminists*. New York: Notes from the Second Year, Inc., 1970. See in addition: Ti- Grace Atkinson, "Radical Feminism" and "The Institution of Sexual Intercourse"; Lucinda Cisler, "On Abortion and Abortion Law"; Roxanne Dunbar, "Female Liberation as the Basis for Social Revolution"; Carol Hanisch, "The Personal is Political"; Joreen, "Bitch Manifesto"; Pat Mainairdi, "The Politics of Housework"; Anselma dell' Olio, "The Founding of the New Feminist Theatre"; Kathie Sarachild, "A Program for Feminist Consciousness Raising"; Meredith Tax, "Woman and Her Mind: The Story of Everyday Life"; Ellen Willis, "Women and the Left."

Flexner, Eleanor. *Century of Struggle: The Women's Rights Movement in the United States*. New York: Atheneum, 1968. Originally published in 1959.

Friedan, Betty. *The Feminine Mystique*. New York: Dell, 1963.

Grahn, Judy. *The Common Woman*. California: The Women's Press Collective, 1970.

Greer, Germaine. *The Female Eunuch*. New York: McGraw-Hill, 1971. Originally published in England, 1970.

• Lerner, Gerda. *The Grimké Sisters from South Carolina: Pioneers for Women's Rights and Abolition*. New York: Shocken Books, 1971. Originally published in 1967.

McAfee, Kathy and Myrna Wood, eds. "Bread and Roses." *Leviathan*. Vol. 1, June 1969.

Millett, Kate. *Sexual Politics*. New York: Doubleday, 1970.

Morgan, Robin, ed. *Sisterhood Is Powerful: An Anthology of Writings from the Women's Liberation Movement.* New York: Random House, 1970.

O'Neill, William L. *Everyone Was Brave: The Rise and Fall of Feminism in America.* Chicago: Quadrangle Books, 1969.

Seaman, Barbara. *The Doctors' Case Against the Pill.* New York: Peter Wyden, 1969.

———. *Free and Female.* New York: Coward, McCann & Geoghegan, 1972.

Solanas, Valerie. *Scum Manifesto.* New York: Olympia Press, 1968.

Steinem, Gloria. "After Black Power, Women's Liberation?" *New York* magazine, 1969.

———. "A Bunny's Tale." *Show Magazine.* 1963.

Wages For Housework: Women Speak Out. Toronto: May Day Rally. Pamphlet, 1969.

Weisstein, Naomi. "Kinder, Kuche and Kirche: Psychology Constructs the Female." *Scientific Psychology and Social Relevance.* New York: Harper & Row, 1971. Originally published by New England Free Press, 1968.

Wittig, Monique. *Les Guerilleres.* New York: Viking Press, 1971. Originally published in France, 1969.

1971-1977

Atkinson, Ti-Grace. *Amazon Odyssey.* New York: Links Books, 1974.

Barreno, Maria Isabel; Horta, Maria Teresa, and Maria Velho de Costa. *The Three Marias: New Portuguese Letters.* Garden City, New York: Doubleday & Company, 1975.

Bengis, Ingrid. *Combat in the Erogeneous Zone.* New York: Alfred A. Knopf, 1972.

Bluh, Bonnie Charles. *Woman to Woman: European Feminists.* New York: Starognbski Press, 1974.

The Boston Women's Health Collective. *Our Bodies, Ourselves.* New York: Simon & Schuster, 1976.

Brown, Rita Mae. *Rubyfruit Jungle.* Plainfield, Utah: Bantam, 1973.

Brownmiller, Susan. *Against Our Will.* New York: Simon & Schuster, 1975.

By and For Women. *The Women's Gun Pamphlet.* Pamphlet, 1975.

Chesler, Phyllis. "Sex Role Stereotyping and Adjustment." *Psychology of Adjustment*. James F. Adams, ed. Holbrook Press, 1973.

————. *Women and Madness*. New York: Doubleday and Co.,1972.

————. "Women and Mental Illness." *Women: Resources for a Changing World*. The Radcliffe Institute, Radcliffe College, October 1972.

Chesler, Phyllis and Emily Jane Goodman. *Women, Money and Power*. New York: William Morrow & Co., 1976.

Connell, Noreen and Cassandra Wilson, eds. *Rape: The First Sourcebook For Women*. New York: Plume Books, New American Library, 1974.

Davis, Elizabeth Gould. *The First Sex*. New York: G. P. Putnam & Sons, 1971.

DeCrow, Karen. *Sexist Justice*. New York: Random House, 1974.

Deming, Barbara and Arthur Kinoy. *Women & Revolution: A Dialogue*. Pamphlet, 1975.

Dreifus, Claudia. *Women's Fate: Raps from a Feminist Consciousness- Raising Group*. New York: Bantam, 1973.

Dworkin, Andrea. *Woman Hating*. New York: E. P. Dutton, 1974.

Ehrenreich, Barbara and Deirdre English. *Witches, Midwives and Nurses: A History of Women Healers*. Pamphlet, 1972.

Fasteau, Marc Feigen. *The Male Machine*. New York: MacGraw-Hill, 1974.

Fernea, Elizabeth Warnock and Basima Qattan Bezirgan. *Middle Eastern Muslim Women Speak*. Austin: University of Texas Press, 1977.

Frankfurt, Ellen. *Vaginal Politics*. New York: Quadrangle Books, 1972.

Freeman, Jo, ed. *Women: A Feminist Perspective*. Palo Alto, Colorado: Mayfield Publishing Company, 1979. Originally published in 1975.

Freire, Paulo. *Pedagony of the Oppressed*. New York: Herder and Herder, 1971.

French, Marilyn. *The Women's Room*. New York: Summit, 1977.

Gluck, Sherna, ed. *From Parlor To Prison: Five American Suffragists Talk about Their Lives*. New York: Vintage Books, 1976.

Gornick, Vivian and B. K. Moran. *Women in a Sexist Society: Studies in Power and Powerlessness*. New York: Basic Books, 1971. See in addition: Phyllis Chesler, "Patient and Patriarch: Women in the Psychotherapeutic Relationship"; Alta, "Pretty"; Una Stannard, "The Mask of Beauty"; Ruby R. Leavitt, "Women in Other Cultures"; Cynthia Ozick, "Women and Creativity: The Demise of the Dancing Dog"; Linda Nochlin, "Why Are There No Great Women Artists?"; Margaret Adams, "The Compassion Trap."

Goulianos, Joan, ed. *By a Woman Writt: Literature from Six Centuries by and about Women.* Baltimore: Penguin Books, 1974.

Grahn, Judy. *Edward the Dyke and Other Poems.* California: The Women's Press Collective, 1971.

Grimstad, Kirsten, and Susan Rennie, eds. *The New Woman's Survival Sourcebook.* New York: Alfred A. Knopf, 1975.

Henley, Nancy M. *Body Politics: Power, Sex, and Non-Verbal Communications.* Englewood Cliffs, New Jersey: Prentice-Hall, 1977.

Hite, Shere. *The Hite Report on Female Sexuality.* New York: Macmillan Publishing Co., 1976.

Johnston, Jill. *Lesbian Nation: The Feminist Solution.* New York: Simon & Schuster, 1973.

Jong, Erica. *Fear of Flying.* New York: Holt, Rinehart, and Winston, 1973.

Katz, Naomi and Nancy Milton, eds. *Fragment from a Lost Diary and Other Stories: Women of Asia, Africa, and Latin America.* New York: Pantheon Books, 1973.

Kingston, Maxine Hong. *The Woman Warrior: Memoirs of a Girlhood among Ghosts.* New York: Vintage Books, 1975.

Koedt, Anne, ed. and Shulamith Firestone, assoc. ed. *Notes from the Third Year: Women's Liberation.* New York: Notes from the Second Year, Inc., 1971. See in addition: Susan Brownmiller, "Speaking Out on Prostitution"; Barbara Burris, "The Fourth World Manifesto"; Dana Densmore, "Independence from Sexual Revolution"; Claudia Dreifus, "The Selling of a Feminist"; Jo Freeman, "The Building of the Guilded Cage"; Judith Hole and Ellen Levine, "The First Feminists"; Pamela Kearon and Barbara Mehrhof, "Rape: An Act of Terror"; Judy Syfers, "Why I Want a Wife."

Lamb, Myrna. *The Mod Donna and Scyklon Z.* New York: Pathfinder Press, 1971.

Lerman, Rhoda. *Call Me Ishtar.* New York: Doubleday, 1973.

Lerner, Gerda, ed. *Black Women in White America: A Documentary History.* New York: Vintage, 1992. Originally published in 1972.

Mackenzie, Midge. *Shoulder to Shoulder.* New York: Alfred A. Knopf, 1975.

Marine, Gene. *A Male Guide to Women's Liberation.* New York: Avon Books, 1972.

Marston, William Moulton. *Wonder Woman*. Introduction by Gloria Steinem. Essay by Phyllis Chesler. New York: Holt, Rinehart and Winston, 1972.

Martin, Del. *Battered Wives*. San Francisco: Glide Publications, 1976.

———. *Battered Wives*. New York: Pocket Books, 1977.

Medea, Andra and Kathleen Thompson. *Against Rape: A Survival Manual for Women: How to Avoid Entrapment and How to Cope with Rape Physically and Emotionally*. New York: Farrar, Straus, and Giroux, 1974.

Mernissi, Fatima. *Beyond the Veil: Male-Female Dynamics in a Modern Muslim Society*. New York: John Wiley and Sons, 1975.

Millett, Kate. *Flying*. New York: Alfred A. Knopf, 1974.

Minai, Naila. *Women and Islam: Tradition and Transition in the Middle East*. New York: Seaview Books, 1981.

Mitchell, Juliet. *Woman's Estate*. New York: Random House, 1971.

Moers, Ellen. *Literary Women*. New York: Doubleday, 1976.

Morgan, Elaine. *The Descent of Woman*. New York: Stein and Day, 1972.

Morrison, Toni. *Sula*. New York: Knopf, 1973.

Oakley, Ann.*The Sociology of Housework*. New York: Pantheon, 1974.

———. *Women's Work: The Housewife, Past and Present*. New York: Pantheon, 1974.

Piercy, Marge. *Small Changes*. New York: Doubleday, 1973.

———. *Woman on the Edge of Time*. New York: Alfred A. Knopf, 1976.

Reed, Evelyn. *Woman's Evolution: From Matriarchal Clan to Patriarchal Family*. New York: Pathfinder's Press, 1975.

Rich, Adrienne. *Of Woman Born: Motherhood as Experience and Institution*. New York: W. W. Norton and Co., 1976.

Ross, Frances D. *Oreo*. New York: Greyfalcon House, 1974

Rowbotham, Sheila. *Women, Resistance, and Revolution:A History of Women and Revolution in the Modern World*. New York: Vintage, 1974.

Rubin, Lillian Breslow. *Worlds of Pain: Life in the Working-Class Family*. New York: Basic Books, 1976.

Ruether, Rosemary Radford, ed. *Religion and Sexism: Images of Women in the Jewish and Christian Traditions*. New York: Simon & Schuster, 1974.

Russ, Joanna. *The Female Man*. New York: Bantam Press, 1975.

Russell, Diana E. H. and Nicole Van de Ven, eds. *The Proceeding of the International Tribunal on Crimes Against Women*. California: Les Femmes, 1976.

Shelly, Martha. *Crossing the DMZ*. California: The Women's Press Collective, 1974.

Shulman, Alix Kates. *Memoirs of an Ex-Prom Queen*. New York: Random House, 1972.

Snodgrass, Jon, ed. *A Book of Readings for Men Against Sexism*. New York: Times Change Press, 1977.

Stannard, Una. *Mrs. Man*.San Francisco: Germain Books, 1977.

Stone, Merlin. *When God Was a Woman*. Great Britain: Virgo Limited, 1976.

Walker, Alice. *Meridian*. New York: Harcourt, Brace and Jovanovich, 1976.

1978-1984

Adler, Margot. *Drawing Down the Moon. Witches, Druids, Goddess- Worshippers, and Other Pagans in America Today*. New York: Viking Press, 1979.

Alpert, Jane. *Growing Up Underground*. New York: William Morrow, 1981.

Anzaldua, Gloria and Cherrie Moraga, eds. *This Bridge Called My Back: Writings by Radical Women of Color*. New York: Kitchen Table, Women of Color Press, 1981.

Armstrong, Louise. *Kiss Daddy Goodnight: A Speak-Out on Incest*. New York: Hawthorn, 1978.

Barry, Kathleen. *Female Sexual Slavery*. Englewood Cliffs, New Jersey: Prentice-Hall, 1979.

Barry, Kathleen, Bunch, Charlotte, and Shirley Castley, eds. *International Feminism: Networking Against Female Sexual Slavery*. New York: The International Women's Tribune Centre, Inc., 1984.

Bernikow, Louise. *Among Women*. New York: Harmony Books, 1980.

Bridenthal, Renate, Grossmann, Atina, and Marion Kaplan, eds. *When Biology Became Destiny: Women in Weimar and Nazi Germany*. New York: Monthly Review Press, 1984.

Broner, E. M. *A Weave of Women*. New York: Holt, Rinehart and Winston, 1978.

Brownstein, Rachel, M. *Becoming a Heroine: Reading About Women in Novels*. New York: Penguin, 1984.

Budapest, Z. *The Holy Book of Women's Mysteries. I & II*. Oakland, California: Self Published, 1976-78.

Bulkin, Elly, Minnie Bruce Pratt, and Barbara Smith. *Yours in Struggle: Three Feminist Perspectives on Anti-Semitism*. Brooklyn, New York: Long Haul Press, 1984.

Chesler, Phyllis. *With Child: A Diary of Motherhood*. New York: Lippincott & Crowell, 1979.

Chicago, Judy. *The Dinner Party: A Symbol of Our Heritage*. Garden City, New York: Anchor Books, 1979.

Chodorow, Nancy. *The Reproduction of Mothering: Psychoanalysis and the Sociology of Gender*. Berkeley: University of California Press, 1978.

Clement, Catherine. *Opera: Or the Undoing of Women*. Minneapolis: The University of Minnesota Press, 1988. Originally published as: *L' opera ou la defaite des femmes*. France: Bernard Grasset, 1979.

Daly, Mary. *GYN/Ecology: The Metaethics of Radical Feminism*. Boston: Beacon Press, 1978.

———. *Pure Lust: Elemental Feminist Philosophy*. Boston: Beacon Press, 1984.

Degler, Carl N. *At Odds: Women and the Family in America From the Revolution to the Present*. Oxford: Oxford University Press, 1980.

Eisenstein, Hester. *Contemporary Feminist Thought*. Boston: G. K. Hall, 1983.

Eisenstein, Zillah R., ed. *Capitalist Patriarchy and the Case for Socialist Feminism*. New York: Monthly Review Press, 1979.

Faderman, Lillian. *Surpassing the Love of Men: Romantic Friendships and Love between Women from the Renaissance to the Present*. New York: William Morrow, 1981.

Farley, Lin. *Sexual Shakedown: The Sexual Harassment of Women on the Job*. New York: McGraw-Hill, 1978.

Fisher, Elizabeth. *Women's Creation: Sexual Evolution and the Shaping of Society*. Garden City, New York: Anchor/Doubleday, 1979.

Fritz, Leah. *Dreamers & Dealers: An Intimate Appraisal of the Women's Movement*. Boston: Beacon Press, 1979.

Giddings, Paula. *When I Where I Enter: The Impact of Black Women on Race and Sex in America*. New York: William Morrow, 1984.

Grahn, Judy. *Another Mother Tongue: Gay Words, Gay Worlds*. Boston: Beacon Press, 1984.

Gilligan, Carol. *In a Different Voice: Psychological Theory and Women's Development*. Cambridge: Harvard University Press, 1982.

Gornick, Vivian. *Essays in Feminism*. New York: Harper & Row, 1978.

Greer, Germaine. *The Obstacle Race: The Fortunes of Women Painters and Their Work*. New York: Farrar, Straus & Giroux, 1979.

Griffen, Susan. *Woman and Nature: The Roaring Inside Her*. New York: Harper & Row, 1978.

Herman, Judith Lewis. *Father-Daughter Incest*. Cambridge: Harvard University Press, 1981.

Hite, Shere. *The Hite Report on Male Sexuality*. New York: Ballantine Books, 1981.

hooks, bell. *Ain't I a Woman: Black Women and Feminism*. Boston: South End Press, 1981.

———. *Feminist Theory from Margin to Center*. Boston: South End Press, 1984.

Hull, Gloria T., Scott, Patricia Bell, and Barbara Smith. *All the Women Are White, All the Blacks Are Men, But Some of Us Are Brave: Black Women's Studies*. Old Westbury, New York: The Feminist Press, 1982.

Johnson, Sonia. *From Housewife to Heretic: One Woman's Struggle for Equal Rights and Her Excommunication from the Mormon Church*. Garden City, New York: Doubleday & Co., 1981.

Jones, Ann. *Women Who Kill*. New York: Holt, Rinehart, and Winston, 1980.

Joseph, Gloria. "Black Mothers and Daughters: Traditional and New Populations." *Sage*. Vol. 1, 1984.

Laska, Vera. *Women in the Resistance and in the Holocaust: The Voices of Eyewitnesses*. Westport: Greenwood Press, 1983.

Lorde, Audre. *Sister Outsider: Essays and Speeches*. Trumansburg, New York: The Crossing Press, 1984.

Luker, Kristin. *Abortion and the Politics of Motherhood*. Berkeley: University of California Press, 1984.

MacKinnon, Catharine A. *Sexual Harassment of Working Women*. New Haven: Yale University Press, 1979.

McAllister, Pam, ed. *Reweaving the Web of Life: Feminism and Nonviolence*. Philadelphia: New Society Publishers, 1982.

Moraga, Cherrie and Gloria Anzaldua, eds. *This Bridge Called My Back: Writings by Radical Women of Color*. Watertown, Massachusetts: Persephone Press, 1981.

Olsen, Tillie. *Silences*. New York: Delacorte Press/Seymour Lawrence, 1978.

Pagels, Elaine. *The Gnostic Gospels*. New York: Random House, 1979.

Pleck, Joseph H. and Robert Brannon, eds. "Male Roles and the Male Experience." *Journal of Social Issues*. Vol. 34, 1978.

Pogrebin, Letty Cottin.*Growing Up Free: Raising Your Child in the 80's*. New York: McGraw-Hill, 1980.

Radl, Shirley Rogers. *The Invisible Woman: Target of the Religious New Right*. New York: Dell, 1983.

Rohrlich, Ruby and Elaine Hoffman Baruch, eds. *Women in Search of Utopia: Mavericks and Mythmakers*. New York: Schocken Books, 1984.

Rose, Phyllis. *Parallel Lives: Five Victorian Marriages*. New York: Alfred A. Knopf, 1983.

Ruddick, Sara. "Maternal Thinking." *Mothering: Essays in Feminist Theory*. Joyce Trebilcot, ed. Totowa, New Jersey: Rowman and Allanheld, 1983.

Ruether, Rosemary, and Eleanor Mclaughlin, eds. *Women of Spirit*. New York: Simon & Schuster, 1979.

Rush, Florence. *The Best Kept Secret: Sexual Abuse of Children*. New Jersey: Prentice-Hall, 1980.

Russ, Joanna. *How to Suppress Women's Writing*. Great Britain: The Women's Press, 1983.

Russell, Diana E. H. *Rape in Marriage*. New York: Macmillan Publishing Co., 1982.

Sargent, Lydia, ed. *Women and Revolution: A Discussion of the Unhappy Marriage of Maxism and Feminism*. Boston: South End Press, 1981.

Schneider, Susan Weidman. *Jewish and Female: Choices and Changes in Our Lives Today*. New York: Simon & Schuster, 1984.

Smith, Barbara, ed. *Home Girls: A Black Feminist Anthology*. New York: Kitchen Table, Women of Color Press, Inc., 1983.

Snitow, Ann, Christine Stansell, and Sharon Thompson, eds. *Powers of Desire: The Politics of Sexuality*. New York: Monthly Review Press, 1983.

Spender, Dale. *There's Always Been a Women's Movement This Century*. London: Pandora, 1983.

———.*Women of Ideas and What Men Have Done to Them from Aphra Behn to Adrienne Rich*. London: Routledge, Kegan and Paul Ltd., 1982.

Starhawk. *The Spiral Dance*. New York: Harper & Row, 1979.

Steinem, Gloria. *Outrageous Acts and Everyday Rebellions*. New York: Holt, Rinehart and Winston, 1983.

Torton Beck, Evelyn, ed. *Nice Jewish Girls: A Lesbian Anthology*. Boston: Beacon Press, 1982.

Walker, Alice. *In Search of Our Mothers' Gardens*. New York: Harcourt Brace Jovanovich, 1983.

———. *The Color Purple*. New York: Harcourt, Brace Jovanovich, 1982.

Walker, Lenore E. *The Battered Woman*. New York: Harper & Row, 1979.

Wallace, Michelle. *Black Macho and the Myth of the Black Super Woman*. New York: The Dial Press, 1978.

1985-1991

Anderson, Bonnie S. and Judith P. Zinsser. *A History of Their Own: Women in Europe from Prehistory to the Present*. 2 vols. New York: Harper and Row, 1988.

Atwood, Margaret. *Cat's Eye*. New York: Doubleday, 1989.

Badran, Margot and Miriam Cooke. *Opening the Gates: A Century of Arab Feminist Writing*. Bloomington, Indiana: Indiana University Press, 1990.

Barry, Kathleen. *Susan B. Anthony: A Biography*. New York and London: New York University Press, 1988.

Bass, Ellen and Laura Davis. *The Courage to Heal: A Guide for Women Survivors of Child Sexual Abuse*. New York: Harper & Row, 1988.

Belenky, Mary Field, Clinchy, Blythe McVicker, Goldenberger, Nancy Rule, and Jill Mattuck Tarule, eds. *Women's Ways of Knowing: The Development of Self, Voice, and Mind*. New York: Basic Books, 1986.

Brant, Beth. *Mohawk Trail*. Ithaca, New York: Firebrand Books, 1985.

Bright, Susie. *Susie Sexperts Lesbian Sex World*. Pittsburg: Cleis Press, 1990.

Budapest, Zsuzsanna E., *The Grandmother of Time*. New York: Harper & Row, 1989.

Caplan, Paula J. *The Myth of Women's Masochism*. New York: E. P. Dutton, 1985.

———. *Don't Blame Mother: Mending the Mother-Daughter Relationship*. New York: Harper & Row, 1989.

Caputi, Jane. *The Age of Sex Crime*. Bowling Green: Bowling Green State University Press, 1987.

Chernin, Kim. *The Hungry Self: Women, Eating, and Identity.* New York: Random House, 1985.

Chesler, Phyllis. "Anorexia Becomes Electra: Women, Eating and Identity." *New York Times Book Review.* 21 July 1985.

———. "Mother-Hatred and Mother-Blaming: What Electra Did to Clytemnestra. Motherhood: A Feminist Perspective." *Journal of Women and Therapy.* Vol. 10, 1990.

———. *Mothers on Trial: The Battle for Children and Custody.* New York: McGraw-Hill, 1986.

———. "Mothers on Trial: The Custodial Vulnerability of Women." *Feminism and Psychology: An International Journal.* Vol. 1, 1991.

———. "Re-examining Freud." *Psychology Today.* September 1989.

———. *Sacred Bond: The Legacy of Baby M.* New York: Times Books/ Random House, 1988.

Curb, Rosemary and Nancy Manahan. *Lesbian Nuns: Breaking the Silence.* Tallahassee: Naiad Press, 1985.

Dworkin, Andrea. *Mercy.* New York: Four Walls Eight Windows, 1991.

Faludi, Susan. *Backlash: The Undeclared War against American Women.* New York: Crown, 1991.

Gilligan, Carol, Jane Victoria Ward, Jill McLean Taylor, and Betty Bardige. *Mapping the Moral Domain: A Contribution of Women's Thinking to Psychological Theory and Education.* Cambridge: Harvard University Press, 1988.

Gornick, Vivian. *Fierce Attachments: A Memoir.* New York: Farrar, Straus & Giroux, 1987.

Gray, Elizabeth Dodson., ed. *Sacred Dimensions of Women's Experience.* Wellesley, Massachusetts: Roundtable Press, 1988.

Harding, Sandra. *Whose Science? Whose Knowledge: Thinking from Women's Lives.* Ithaca, New York: Cornell University Press, 1991.

Hoffman, Merle. "Beyond the Laws of Men." *On the Issues.* Winter 1991.

———. "Know and Use Your Enemies." *On the Issues.* Vol. 13, 1989.

hooks, bell. *Talking back: Thinking Feminist, Thinking Black.* Boston: South End Press, 1989.

Jeffreys, Sheila. *The Spinster and Her Enemies: Feminism and Sexuality, 1880-1930.* London: Pandora, 1985.

Jones, Jacqueline. *Labor of Love, Labor of Sorrow: Black Women, Work, and the Family from Slavery to the Present.* New York: Basic Books, 1985.

Johnson, Buffie. *Lady of the Beasts: Ancient Images of the Goddess and Her Sacred Animals*. New York: Harper & Row, San Francisco, 1988.

Karlsen, Carol F. *The Devil in the Shape of a Woman: Witchcraft in Colonial New England*. New York: W.W. Norton, 1987.

Kaye/Kantrowitz, Melanie and Irena Klepfisz, eds. *The Tribe of Dina: A Jewish Women's Anthology*. Montpelier, Vermont: Sinister Wisdom Books, 1986. Originally published in *Sinister Wisdom*, 1986.

Jones, Jacqueline. *Labor of Love, Labor of Sorrow: Black Women, Work and the Family from Slavery to the Present*. New York: Basic Books, 1985.

Lobel, Kerry, ed. *Naming the Violence: Speaking Out About Lesbian Battering*. The National Coalition Against Domestic Violence Lesbian Task Force. Seattle: Seal Press, 1986.

MacKinnon, Catharine A. *Feminism Unmodified: Discourses on Life and Law*. Cambridge: Harvard University Press, 1987.

———. *Toward a Feminist Theory of the State*. Cambridge: Harvard University Press, 1989.

Margolies, Eva. *The Best of Friends, The Worst of Enemies: Women's Hidden Power over Women*. New York: The Dial Press, 1985.

McAllister, Pam. *You Can't Kill the Spirit*. Philadelphia: New Society Publishers, 1988.

Miner, Valerie and Helen Longino, eds. *Competition: A Feminist Taboo?* New York: The Feminist Press, 1987.

Pogrebin, Letty Cottin. *Deborah, Golda and Me*. New York: Crown, 1991.

Raven, Arlene. *Crossing Over: Feminism and Art of Social Concerns*. Ann Arbor, Michigan: UMI Research Press, 1988.

Raymond, Janice G. *A Passion for Friends: Toward a Philosophy of Female Affection*. Boston: Beacon Press, 1986.

Russ, Joanna. *Magic Mommas, Trembling Sisters, Puritans & Perverts: Feminist Essays*. Trumansberg, New York: The Crossing Press, 1985.

Sjoo, Monica and Barbara Mor. *The Great Cosmic Mother: Rediscovering the Religion of the Earth*. San Francisco: Harper & Row, 1987.

Spender, Dale. *For the Record*. London: The Women's Press Limited, 1985.

Walker, Barbara G. *The Skeptical Feminist: Discovering the Virgin, Mother and Crone*. San Francisco: Harper & Row, 1987.

Walker, Lenore, E. *Terrifying Love: Why Battered Women Kill and How Society Responds*. New York: Harper & Row, 1989.

Wittig, Monique. *Crossing the Acheron*. London: Peter Owen, 1987. First published in French, 1985.

Wolf, Naomi. *The Beauty Myth*. New York: William Morrow, 1991.

1992-1997

Afkhami, Mahnaz. *Faith and Freedom: Women's Human Rights in the Muslim World*. Syracuse, New York: Syracuse University Press, 1995

Allison, Dorothy. *Skin: Talking About Sex, Class & Literature*. Ithaca, New York: Firebrand Books, 1994.

Antonelli, Judith, S. "Beyond Nostalgia: Rethinking the Goddess," *On the Issues*. Vol. 6, 1997.

Armstrong, Louise. "Who Stole Incest?" *On the Issues*. Fall 1994.

Bernikow, Louise. *American Woman's Almanac*. New York: Berkeley-Putnam, 1996.

Cantor, Aviva. *Jewish Women, Jewish Men: The Legacy of Patriarchy in Jewish Life*. San Francisco: Harper San Francisco, 1995.

Caplan, Paula J. *Lifting a Ton of Feathers: A Woman's Guide to Surviving in the Academic World*. Toronto: University of Toronto Press, 1992.

———. *They Say You're Crazy: How the World's Most Powerful Psychiatrists Decide Who Is Normal*. Reading, Massachusettes: Addison Wesley, 1995.

———. "Try Diagnosing Men's Mind Games Instead of Pathologizing Women." *On the Issues*. Winter 1997.

Carlip, Hillary. *Girl Power: Young Women Speak Out!* New York: Warner Books, 1995.

Chadwick, Whitney, and Isabelle de Courtivron. *Significant Others: Creativity & Intimate Partnership*. London: Thames and Hudson, 1993.

Chesler, Ellen. *Woman of Valor: Margaret Sanger and the Birth Control Movement in America*. New York: Simon & Schuster, 1992.

Chesler, Phyllis. "Custody Determinations: Gender Bias in the Courts." Barbara Katz Rothman, ed. *Encyclopedia of Childbearing: Critical Perspectives*. Phoenix: Oryx Press, 1992.

———. "The Dead Man is Not on Trial." *On the Issues*. Winter 1994.

———. "A Double Standard for Murder?" *New York Times OP-ED*. 9 January 1992.

———. "Heroism is Our Only Alternative." A Response to a Retrospective on *Women and Madness*. *The Journal of Feminism and Psychology*. Vol. 4, May 1994.

———. "The Men's Auxiliary: Protecting the Rule of the Fathers." *Women Respond to the Men's Movement*. Kay Leigh Hagan, ed. San Francisco: Harper San Francisco, 1992.

———. *Patriarchy: Notes of an Expert Witness*. Monroe, Maine: Common Courage Press, 1994.

———. "Sexual Violence Against Women and a Woman's Right to Self-Defense: The Case of Aileen Carol Wuornos." *St. John's University Law Review*. Fall-Winter 1993 and *Criminal Practice Law Report*. Vol. 1, October 1993.

———. "The Shellshocked Woman." *New York Times Book Review*. 23 August 1992.

———. "What is Justice for a Rape Victim." *On the Issues*. Winter 1995.

———. "When a 'Bad' Woman Kills: The Trials of Aileen Wuornos." *On the Issues*. Summer 1992.

———. "When They Call You Crazy." *On the Issues*. Summer 1994.

Chesler, Phyllis, Rothblum, Esther D., and Ellen Cole, eds. *Feminist Foremothers in Women's Studies, Psychology, and Mental Health*. Binghamton, New York: The Haworth Press , 1995.

Copelon, Rhonda. "Surfacing Gender: Reconceptualizing Crimes Against Women in Time of War." *Mass Rape: The War Against Women in Bosnia-Herzegovina*. Alexandra Stiglymyer, ed. Lincoln and London: University of Nebraska Press, 1992.

Daly, Meg, ed. *Surface Tensions: Love, Sex, and Politics between Lesbians and Straight Women*. New York: Touchstone, 1996.

Derricotte, Toi. *The Black Notebook*. New York: W. W. Norton, 1997.

Dusky, Lorraine. *Still Unequal: The Shameful Truth about Women and Justice in America*. New York: Crown Publishers, 1996.

Dutton, Donald G. and Susan K. Golant. *The Batterer: A Psychological Profile*. New York: Basic Books, 1995.

Dworkin, Andrea. *Letters from a War Zone*. Chicago: Lawerence Hill Books, 1993.

Estés, Clarissa Pinkola. *Women Who Run with the Wolves: Myths and Stories of the Wild Woman Archetype*. New York: Ballantine Books, 1992.

Findlen, Barbara, ed. *Listen Up. Voices from the Next Feminist Generation*. Seattle: Seal Press, 1995.

Freyd, Jennifer J. *Betrayal Trauma.* Cambridge: Harvard University Press, 1995.

Geller, Jeffrey L. and Maxine Harris. *Women of the Asylum: Voices from Behind the Walls 1840-1945.* New York: Bantam Doubleday Dell Publishing Group, 1994. Introduction by Phyllis Chesler.

Gordon, Linda. *Pitied But Not Entitled: Single Mothers and the History of Welfare.* Cambridge: Harvard University Press, 1994.

Herman, Judith Lewis. *Trauma and Recovery.* New York: Basic Books, 1992.

Hite, Shere. *Women as Revolutionary Agents of Change: The Hite Report and Beyond.* Wisconsin: The University of Wisconsin Press,1993.

Hoffman, Merle. "Facing the Dragon: Reflections on Female Heroism." *On the Issues.* Winter 1997.

———."Happiness and the Feminist Mind." *On the Issues.* Fall 1996.

———. "Praise the Lord and Kill the Doctor." *On the Issues.* Summer 1994.

Jeffreys, Sheila. *The Lesbian Heresy: A Feminist Perspective on the Lesbian Sexual Revolution.* Australia: Spinifex, 1993.

Kimmel, Michael S., and Thomas E. Mosmiller. *Against the Tide: Pro-Feminist Men in the United States 1776-1990.* Boston: Beacon Press, 1992.

Nestle, Joan, ed. *The Persistent Desire: A Butch-Femme Reader.* Boston: Alyson, 1992.

Orenstein, Peggy. *Schoolgirls: Young Women, Self-Esteem, and the Confidence Gap.* New York: Anchor Books, 1994.

Painter, Nell Irvin. *Sojourner Truth: A Life, A Symbol.* New York: W.W. Norton, 1996.

Pelka, Fred. "Raped: A Male Survivor Breaks His Silence." *On the Issues.* Spring 1992.

Penelope, Julia, ed. *Out of the Class Closet: Lesbians Speak.* Freedom, California.: The Crossing Press, 1994.

Pipher, Mary. *Reviving Ophelia: Saving the Selves of Adolescent Girls.* New York: Ballantine Books. 1994.

Pope, Kenneth S. "Scientific Research, Recovered Memory, and Context: Seven Surprising Findings." *Women and Therapy.* Vol. 19, 1996.

Radford, Jill and Diana E. H. Russell, eds. *Femicide: The Politics of Woman Killing.* New York: Macmillan Publishing Co., 1992.

Raven, Arlene. "Judy Chicago: The Artist Critics Love to Hate." *On the Issues.* Vol. 3, 1994.

Rivers, Diana. *Daughters of the Great Star.* Boston: Lace Publications, 1992.

Russ, Joanna. *What Are We Fighting for? Sex, Race, Class, and the Future of Feminism.* New York: St. Martin's Press, 1997.

Sapinsley, Barbara. *The Private War of Mrs. Packard.* New York: Kodansha, 1995. Introduction by Phyllis Chesler.

Steinem, Gloria. *Moving Beyond Words.* New York: Simon & Schuster, 1994.

Stiglymyer, Alexandra, ed. "The Rapes in Bosnia-Herzegovina." *Mass Rape: The War Against Women in Bosnia-Herzegovina.* Lincoln and London: University of Nebraska Press, 1992.

Templin, Charlotte. *Feminism and the Politics of Literary Reputation: The Example of Erica Jong.* Lawrence, Kansas: University of Kansas Press, 1995.

Walker, Rebecca, ed. *To Be Real: Telling the Truth and Changing the Face of Feminism.* New York: Anchor Books, 1995.

Weiner, Kayla and Arinna Moon, eds. *Jewish Women Speak Out: Expanding the Boundaries Of Psychology.* Foreword by Phyllis Chesler. Seattle: Canopy Press, 1995.

Wood, Mary Elene. *The Writing on the Wall: Women's Autobiography and the Asylum.* Chicago: University of Illinois Press, 1994.

Young-Bruehl, Elisabeth. *The Anatomy of Prejudices.* Cambridge: Harvard University Press, 1996.

FEMINIST NEWSPAPERS, MAGAZINES, AND JOURNALS

Calx
Chrysalis
Heresies
Matriarch's Way: Journal of Female Supremacy
Ms.
Off Our Backs
On the Issues
Signs
Sojourner